FADED GLAMOUR
by the Sea

FADED GLAMOUR
by the Sea

PEARL LOWE

WITH SPECIAL PHOTOGRAPHY BY DAVE WATTS

CICO BOOKS

LONDON NEW YORK

Published in 2022 by CICO Books
An imprint of Ryland Peters & Small Ltd
20–21 Jockey's Fields   341 E 116th St
London WC1R 4BW   New York, NY 10029

www.rylandpeters.com

10 9 8 7 6 5 4 3 2 1

A CIP catalog record for this book is available from
the Library of Congress and the British Library.

ISBN: 978 1 80065 1012

Printed in China

Photography: Dave Watts, Amy Neunsinger (pages
196-205) and Helena Christensen (pages 96-105)

Art director: Rachel Ashwell

Words by: Natasha Garnett

Endpapers: Morton, Young & Borland Textiles

Editor: Sophie Devlin

In-house art director: Sally Powell

Head of production: Patricia Harrington

Senior commissioning editor: Annabel Morgan

Publisher: Cindy Richards

Contents

Introduction

It has always been a lifelong dream of mine to have a house by the sea. I'm not sure what it is about the call of the sea that I find so compelling, but it is as though I am magnetically drawn to it. The sound of the waves breaking onto a reef, the sight of the tides rebounding and receding, the smell of salt water... all of these experiences do wonders for my body and soul.

I have a deep affinity for water and ever since I moved away from London in 2005 I have always lived close to it – be that by a river or even just a stream – but as soothing as that is, I still found myself longing for the waves and have yearned to have a bolthole of my own on the coast.

It was fantasy of mine, shared by my husband Danny Goffey, and a subject that would inevitably resurface every summer when we took our four children – Daisy, Alfie, Frankie and Betty – to the sea for our annual getaway. "Wouldn't it be wonderful to have a house here?", was the refrain as we sat on the beach and watched them play in the waves.

We both knew back then that this was just wishful thinking. But last year that little pipe dream became a reality when we took possession of an enchanting wooden house on the south coast of England.

We had, finally, taken the plunge.

Opposite The exterior of my house by the sea is adorned with this extraordinary and enchanting mosaic of shells and pebbles collected from the beach, which lies at the bottom of our garden. The house, on the coast of East Sussex, was built in the 1940s and this mural, which wraps around the ground floor of the two-storey house, was created by an artist who lived here all those years ago. It tells the story of the local area and of her life here by the sea. I think this is the reason why I fell in love with the property when I saw it for the first time.

Back in the day, when we dreamt of our fantasy coastal home, I think we both imagined that it would be in warmer climes. As a result of our careers, Danny, as the drummer in the band Supergrass, and I, in my work as a designer, have been lucky enough to travel to some of the most exotic locations in the world and our family holidays were usually to some idyllic Mediterranean isle.

But when it came to eventually finding our house by the sea, we both knew that we wanted to be be here in the British Isles. Maybe that's a sign of getting older and, perhaps, wiser. To be honest, plane travel no longer holds that same allure it once did when I was footloose and fancy free. And these days I am more conscious of my carbon footprint, too. When Danny and I set out on this journey, we soon realized that we didn't just want a house by the sea, we wanted it to be a *home* by the sea. It should be a place for family and friends to gather or where we could just be alone with our dogs.

We didn't want a sterile villa that we would only visit in season. We wanted to use it all year round, come rain or shine, and most importantly of all, for me at least, it would be a place I could put my mark on because this was going to be our retreat, our home from home. And so it was that we ended up here in East Sussex, just a stone's throw from one of the loveliest beaches I have ever seen.

I have always had quite a nostalgic love of the British coast, which I think is often overlooked in our quest to find the exotic. But for me, it makes my heart sing. Think of all the majestic Victorian and Edwardian hotels on the promenades of our coastal towns. The rows of beach huts, painted in vibrant sherbet and ice-cream hues that line our shores. Then there are fish and chip shops, the rickety shacks, the cafes, the piers, those wonderful old guesthouses.

All of this appeals to my aesthetic – a sense of faded glamour, a style that I would describe as a mix of the gloriously decadent yet well-lived in. It is elegant but whimsical, eclectic but well thought-out. In my last book, *Faded Glamour*, I took you on a tour of some of the inspiring houses that I felt embodied that look. Now I am going to take you to the coast to visit properties, which I believe play with this theme.

We start in the south-east of England, where I gained inspiration for my own home, from a magical beach hut to a disused railway carriage that has been converted into a family home. We will visit a recently refurbished guesthouse with a rock-n-roll vibe before venturing further afield to an enchanting beach house in Denmark and a Malibu property that overlooks the Pacific Ocean.

Each of these properties, diverse as they are, has been a great source of inspiration when it came to creating my own slice of faded glamour by the sea.

Opposite I'm always on the hunt for a great vintage find – furniture, fabrics and textiles, papers, artworks and objects. I love browsing antique markets and brocantes in my quest to find unique pieces that are the essence of faded glamour. One of my favourite go-to stores is Old Albion in the Dorset town of Bridport, which is pictured here. This fabulous emporium is run by Sharon Bradley, who has the most exquisite taste when it comes to antique furniture and other retro items. I find it impossible to leave here without making a purchase of some sort, from French dressers/ hutches and school chairs, armchairs and sofas to decorative glass domes and neon lights.

My Faded Glamour by the Sea

From the moment when I first set eyes on this house,
I knew that I had found my dream property by the
sea. I didn't even need set foot inside it to know this was
the one. There was just something so enchanting about
it that made my heart skip. I looked toward my husband
Danny as we got out of the car and saw that he was
smiling too. We'd finally found it.

Opposite The first room I worked on when we moved here was the kitchen, simply because this was going to be the space that needed the most work. The house was already divine when we bought it, but it did need updating. Once all the building work was finished and we were ready to make a start on the interiors, one of my first purchases was this beautiful vintage-style mouth-blown glass pendant light from Rothschild & Bickers. By day it looks like an exquisite amber gem, and at night it gives off the softest and warmest of glows, which brings a sultry ambience to the room.

Overleaf With its vaulted ceiling and French windows that lead out into the garden, this room is filled with the most beautiful light. I wanted to make the most of it by painting the tongue-and-groove panelling in the palest shade – here I have used Pointing by Farrow & Ball. For the kitchen cabinets, I turned to DeVol and went for this Shaker design, which I feel is in keeping with the style of the property. The cooker/stove is from Bertazzoni. I'm a firm believer that the greatest investment you can make when you buy a house is a good kitchen. It should be not only functional but also aesthetically pleasing because, after all, this is the room in which we are likely to spend the majority of our time nowadays.

It had been a long journey to get here, not just physically – it takes a good three hours in the car to travel from our house in Somerset to East Sussex – but also emotionally, because for so many years Danny and I had debated on the pros and cons of buying a retreat by the sea. Was it really what we wanted; could we afford it; was this the right move for us as a family?

But when we saw this two-storey, clapboard house for the first time our minds were made up. It was everything we wanted. Hidden away down a bumpy dirt track, it was secluded and, as such, offered us the sense of peace and tranquillity we longed for. It was romantic, it had character, it was quirky and, best of all, it was just a pebble's throw from one of the most beautiful beaches in the British Isles.

Within hours of that viewing we made an offer.

I have been lucky enough to travel the globe and visit some of the finest resorts there are. However, when I think of the sea, I am not picturing white sandy beaches or crystal clear, turquoise waters in tropical climes or even in the Mediterranean. Enticing as that may be for a week or two, I admit I'm not very good on vacation – I get restless, as all my children can attest. It has become something of a running joke in the family that none of them even bothers to unpack when we go abroad, knowing that I'm quite likely to turn on my heel as soon as we've arrived and will want to find somewhere else to stay.

Left Although I wanted the kitchen to be quite simple in its design, I was keen to imbue it with character. This space is roomy enough for us to cook and entertain, but there is not very much storage space. I also had to consider the fact that, as a self-confessed serial hoarder, I have quite a lot of "stuff", as Danny calls it, so I needed to think creatively. Across the beam I have installed this brass rail, from which I can hang teacups, pots, jugs/pitchers and, as seen here, my set of vintage china napkin rings. Not only has this freed up much-needed drawer space, but stringing them in this way makes them look like a little garland.

Opposite At this end of the kitchen, a pair of French windows leads out into the garden. I have dressed them with lace curtains, something of a signature look of mine. I love to use lace panels as window coverings, not just because they are beautiful but because they let in the light while creating shade when you need it. I also enjoy how this fine fabric allows for the sea breeze to waft in on balmy nights. As someone who loves to collect glass and tableware, I would find it almost criminal to hide it away so I love this vintage cabinet that hangs above the peach-coloured marble counter. The doors of the glass-fronted cupboards below are lined in the finest of muslins.

That's not because I no longer have a sense of wanderlust, but recently I've found I don't necessarily have to board a plane to satisfy it. Sometimes your sense of paradise is right there on your doorstep, maybe just a few counties away, as I discovered as I explored this part of the country. And when I fantasized about a life by the sea, it had always been here in England because that is where my heart lies.

My love of the British seaside began when I was a little girl when my paternal grandmother, Nana Betty, used to take me on day trips from London to Eastbourne and Brighton to visit her friends.

Opposite The open-plan living space at the bottom of the house extends from the kitchen and dining area to the sitting room. In order to maximize on the flow of this area, which I love, I used the same pale paint colour throughout, from the tongue-and-groove walls to the stripped floorboards. However, I decided not to paint the original woodwork that surrounds the windows and doorways on this floor, because I wanted to retain a sense of the history of the house. The charming floral antique bucket chair is from one of my favourite stores, Lark Vintage, in my hometown of Frome, Somerset. The artworks on the wall were mostly sourced from the internet. In the background is a lovely Italianate piece of furniture that I found in a market, which serves as a drinks cabinet.

I loved those outings, which I remember very clearly to this day. My grandmother had a gaggle of girlfriends and they would be all dolled up in their 1950s-style Sunday best, with their bleached, bouffant hairstyles and bright pink lipstick, smelling of a heady mix of Yardley perfume and talcum powder. They used to smother me with attention and feed me fish and chips and ice creams while they gossiped the afternoon away in their deckchairs. Then we would all saunter down to the pier, where I would be further indulged with a jaw-cracking, teeth-rotting stick of rock, much to my mother's horror.

Above Although I'm quite spiritual by nature, I am not remotely religious, and yet I find myself drawn to iconography, especially when it comes to the Virgin Mary. Perhaps it has something to do with my maternal instinct, but I find images of the Madonna and Child incredibly soothing and I simply can't resist adorning our homes with them. This causes Danny to joke that he sometimes feels as though he is living in a convent.

Previous pages When it comes to the interior design of our homes, Danny pretty much gives me carte blanche. After all these years together, we share the same aesthetic, so he trusts me to take the lead – with one exception. The area where he does insist on taking control is the hanging of our artwork. It's a task I am more than happy to relinquish to him, as he has such a good curatorial eye. On this wall of the sitting room, an eclectic mix of oils, nudes, framed drawings and prints surrounds a boxed case containing a taxidermy bird. To the right – as a nod to his love of music – is a framed photograph of two of his icons, Serge Gainsbourg and Jane Birkin. To the left, on the far wall above the French cabinet, homage is paid to the ultimate rock chick, Debbie Harry.

Opposite I love the original porthole doors in the downstairs of the property, as they give the house a maritime feel. I bought the French cabinet online, intending for it to be a piece of furniture on which we could place our television. However, I slightly got the dimensions wrong and it proved to be too tall, as we realized that first night when we had to crane our necks to see the screen. But it was a happy mistake, as it now looks perfect here.

Those childhood memories have stuck with me ever since. When I think of the sea, I remember vividly the faded grandeur of the promenades, the wonderment of the bright, flashing lights of the arcades, the giddy magic of the twirling carousels, the candyfloss/cotton candy stalls and tea shacks and the brass bands playing their ta-ra-ra boom-de-ay, rom-pom-pom tunes.

As the old song goes, "I do like to be by the seaside, I do like to be beside the sea…"

And, now, here I was again.

Above I found this wonderfully battered old leather sofa at The Old Cinema in Chiswick, London. It is an incredible salesroom that specializes in the most fabulous antique, vintage and retro one-off finds. I always try to visit when I am in town. The sofa was a birthday present for Danny.

Opposite Even though the main living area is open plan, I wanted to create distinctive seating areas within it. This sofa, covered in a soft pale linen, is from Graham and Green. As much as I love vintage furniture, I don't like to scrimp when it comes to comfort. So, when buying sofas and beds, with a few exceptions, I tend to be drawn to newer items. This is certainly a piece that you can sink into, without the fear of a random spring prodding you in the back. The multi-coloured blanket, which I adore, preserves the cover from my dogs' muddy paws – they have yet to learn that sofas are off limits. Again, I've used lace panels to shade the windows here. The one pictured here towards the back of the room is a vintage find. On the right, I've used a lace panel from my own collection.

Set in an acre of land within a nature reserve on the coast of East Sussex, the house is just a five-minute walk from the shingle beach and its silvery waves and the nearest town is a quick cycle away, easily accessible for groceries, ice creams and cafes. I could imagine myself taking long coastal walks with the dogs and rejuvenating early-morning dips in the sea. We would have picnics on the beach when the weather was good and there would be day trips to the neighbouring towns, where I would be able to relive the seaside outings of my childhood. But it wasn't just the location, it was the house itself and the story behind it that appealed to me.

Above When I relax on a sofa, I need my cup of tea and and books to be within easy reach. This French-style reproduction coffee table, which I found in Brighton, affords me that luxury. I could lie here all afternoon, plumped up on my array of cushions, feeling the breeze and listening to the sounds of the sea. The tiny ship-in-a-bottle was bought locally and always makes me smile.

Left When decorating a house, my first priority is lighting, because that is what makes a room. A twinkling chandelier hanging from the ceiling at once adds magic to even to the plainest of spaces. A 1920s standing lamp and a silk shade adorned with a cascade of fringe will create glamour and take you back to another era. A sweet little lamp, which you might normally assign to your nightstand, can create warmth on a kitchen counter. I often buy vintage lamps on a whim just because I adore them and then get them rewired, which actually doesn't cost that much. This French glass lamp is from Lark Vintage – I love the crystal beads that hang from its pretty pink shade.

Opposite I can't resist a chandelier. When I found this one on Ebay, I knew it would be perfect to hang from the vaulted ceiling in the kitchen. I love the way the sweet tiny porcelain flowers are entwined into its drop. It reminds me of the rambling, climbing roses in my garden in Somerset. When I can't find the perfect vintage chandelier, I often turn to online retailers such as Ebay and Etsy, which usually have an incredible range of affordable lighting.

Dating back to the 1940s, the house was built by a returning soldier as a gift for his wife, who was an artist and, like me, had a passion for the sea. Back then it was nothing more than a simple yet charming bungalow, but the artist threw stardust at it by embellishing the exterior of the property with a mosaic of shells, This grotto-like mural pays homage to the history of the local area and the couple's life together.

People often ask me why I am so drawn to all things vintage. Aside from the aesthetic, I have great respect for the craftsmanship and fine handiwork of those bygone years, which is slightly lost on us today.

Previous pages Although I wanted the palette of the living areas to be as pale as possible, I felt that the bedrooms should have a warmer feel. Here, in the downstairs spare room, I have used Farrow & Ball's Setting Plaster. It is a colour that works well in the sunlight and at night makes the room feel cozy. The linen curtains are in a fabric called Genevieve by Kate Forman and I love their timeless appearance. The Victorian brass bed is from Susannah Brocante and I love the *Bedknobs and Broomsticks* magic of it. I've dressed it in the most sumptuous mustard-coloured velvet bedspread from Toast and an antique Kantha running-stitched bedcover. The swirl cushion was designed by my friend – and one of my favourite designers – Sera Hersham-Loftus for her eponymous brand Sera of London.

Opposite I love to have flowers around me, in as many rooms I can – I even like to place them on my bath rack! That may sound eccentric, but it's no different to lighting a scented candle when you want to indulge in a long, hot soak. I'm a keen gardener but I have yet to establish my garden here, so I find myself on relying on The Real Flower Company to create wonderful wild posies and bunches of heady blooms with which I can fill the house.

This craftsmanship can often be found in vintage clothing, furniture, linens and lace. But for me, its also about the backstory and this house, with its romantic history, offered that to me in spades.

It was never our intention to make a permanent move to the coast. For the past six years, our family home has been a beautiful Georgian property in Frome, Somerset, a county that we love. I very much doubt that we will leave that yellow sandstone house until we really have to, perhaps when the stairs get to be too much for us. The only downside of our life there is that it is also where Danny and I both have our work.

Above I bought this funny little telephone for a couple of pounds in a local car-boot/yard sale, just because I liked the look of it. Much to my amazement, it actually works, too. Not that my children would understand that – they are of the generation that tends to be confounded by the idea of a landline.

I have my design rooms where I work on my fashion and interiors collections and Danny has his studio, where he writes and records his music. What we wanted was a place we could escape to when we needed a break from the daily rigmarole of our lives.

That said, I was always adamant that this should be a home from home. I didn't want it to have the soulless feeling of holiday rental or a villa abroad. I wanted it to be full of character, our things and our combined aesthetic. While the two properties are so different in terms of architectural style, space and location, I feel that somehow I have achieved that. This is my take on faded glamour, now by the sea.

In terms of the structure of the property, there was, thankfully, little to do. Following the passing of the artist and her husband, the next owners had added to the original bungalow an upper storey, clad in clapboard. This allows for four bedrooms within the house, plus a charming, self-contained cabin. Complete with a kitchen, living area and bathroom, this can accommodate two couples. There is enough room for our brood, as well as friends, without us all being on top of one another. In my mind, this is the key to a perfect holiday.

The interior of the property was going to need a lot of work, as we were soon to discover, much to our dismay. Having left London more than 15 years ago on our quest to find the perfect rural retreat, we were serial movers until we at last found our house in Somerset. I've almost lost count of all the houses we have lived in over the years.

Opposite I love freestanding bathtubs. If you are canny, you find old ones on the internet or in reclamation yards. I get them re-enamelled and then paint the base myself in fun colours. For new tubs, I always turn to Burlington. The blue and white tiles are by Bert & May and the shell motif on the wall was created by the artist who lived here in the 1940s.

Above left I found this charming old mirror at Lark Vintage in Frome. It has a Venetian look to it, which I adore, so I have adorned it with a rather mad, pink-feathered plume to give it a carnival feel.

Above centre This box frame is one of my creations. The toy rabbits belonged to Betty when she was little and, for sentimental reasons, I was loath to throw them away when she grew out of them. They have now become a work of art.

Above right This beautiful 1920s mirrored shelving cabinet was a recent find. Not only do I love the intricacy of its frame and its glamorous appearance, it is also a useful addition to the bathroom. I have used the shelves to display my array of antique glass bottles and a Fornasetti scented candle in one of the brand's iconic ceramic pots.

Previous pages I chose a shade of French grey for the walls of the second spare room in the main house. I have added colour with the fabrics and textiles I selected for the room, including the vintage floral curtains, which I found in Frome. I collect vintage lace and design my own window coverings, as well as tablecloths, for my own interiors collection, but this window is dressed with a panel that I bought via Etsy. This antique bed, upholstered in a fine ticking, is from The French House.

Opposite I bought this antique ornate Florentine chest of drawers from Shepton Mallet flea market. I have a soft spot when it comes to royal memorabilia, hence the commemorative cup that I have filled with flowers and this print of the Queen, which was issued to mark her coronation in 1953 – I found it at Old Albion in Bridport. The reclaimed radiator towards the left I bought online. When we moved in, our first job was to sort out the heating, which had been working on bio-mass fuel. I'm a great believer in anything that it is good for the environment but we did need to update the heating system to make the house habitable. These old radiators have proven to be the perfect solution.

Still, you'd think by now we might have got the hang of moving in terms of reading the small print when it comes to signing a contract but, in our excitement at securing the house, neither of us realized it was off-grid. And by that I'm not talking about there being a wobbly internet connection that the children would scream about, either. The house was bio-mass fuelled, so the heating and the plumbing, as well as the electricity were not exactly what we were used to.

"Pearl! What have we done?" Danny said, with a look of horror on his face as we made our way to bed on our first night in the house.

Above Above the bed I have hung this sweet, little oil of a posy of flowers which I bought from Old Albion. I'm not quite sure what charms me more, the painting itself or the frame, but what I do know is that it looks perfect in this room.

Opposite The main living area of the house is open plan but off it I have created an all-important snug, a little space to which we retreat when we want to read in silence or watch movies and escape the wonderful but slightly relentless chaos of a full house. This sumptuous and opulent red velvet Alice sofa is from Soho Home. The cushions on the sofa are from Geminola. I papered the walls and ceiling to give this area a cozy, homely feel and have separated it off from the main living area using a crocheted curtain.

"We've basically bought a glorified shed!" I use the word "bed" lightly here – our mattress still hadn't arrived, so we would be sleeping on the floor. We had no curtains, no heating, no hot water and no kitchen. We were basically camping, in February, and it was snowing outside.

Thankfully, my husband is understanding and I like to think I'm also quite resourceful when it comes to finding the right person for the right job. Two incredible local electricians, Al and Tom, took the house forward into the 21st century and my brilliant plumber Joe saved us from hypothermia. All we had to do now was deal with the interior.

Above I found this Baroque-style marble-topped side table in Leeds. At first, when I brought it home, I wasn't sure about it and was even tempted to resell it, but in this room I found the perfect place for it. The paper I have used on the walls here is from Morris & Co and is called Daisy. I tend to go to this brand for wallpapers, not just because of their iconic William Morris prints but because they have a wonderfully vintage feel to them that you don't find when you look at the digitally produced papers on the market today.

Opposite I covered the staircase here in a striped flatweave runner from Roger Oates Design. I've been using runners from this brand in my houses for years now. They are of excellent quality and can withstand wear and tear, and I love the wide range of designs.

Overleaf A view of our bedroom at the top of the house. I wanted this room to have a relaxed feel and yet be decadent at the same time. The antique bed frame is from the Three Angels in Brighton. The green bed linen is from Piglet in Bed. And then to add glamour to the room I went to Preen Home for this fabulous fabric to cover the bedhead and for this gorgeous Harlequin silk quilted eiderdown.

Page 42 I have always worn vintage since I was a teenager, long before it was fashionable. Sometimes I find myself drawn to an item, such as this pair of silver boots, simply because I love the design. I then use these pieces as inspiration for my own collection or just as decorative items. The boots are too small for me, but they do fit Betty, which I realized when they kept going missing from my room.

Page 43 This pretty pink floral porcelain vase on my Florentine bedside table was a gift from a friend and is a much-cherished item of mine. I always find it uplifting to have flowers by my bed, especially if they are scented – these heady roses came from my favourite florist, The Real Flower Company.

Above A detail of a beautifully painted lamp in the snug, which here I've paired with a 1920s-style fringed silk shade. Lighting is important to me when it comes to my decorative style, but it can often be expensive. I like to buy a lamp base, from a flea market, and then find a shade to fit it without worrying about whether the styles match.

For that, I turned to my trusted builder Rich, who had previously worked on our house in Somerset. We moved him into our cabin and within just three months, with great skill and craft, he lovingly restored the house to its former glory while also making the changes we needed. Thanks to this amazing team, the house was ready and I had a blank canvas that I could work with.

When it comes to interior design, I've always believed that you must be sympathetic to the house and its location before you go wild. Here, I wanted to preserve the simplicity and serenity of the house.

Pages 44-45 To make the most of the limited space we had on the top floor of the house, we decided not to create a cramped, boxy ensuite bathroom. Instead, I installed this freestanding bathtub at one end of our bedroom and then painted the base in a calming sage hue. To the side of the tub is the most fabulous gold figurine of a cherub – a present from my mother Leila, who is also a designer. The Art Deco mirror was found for me by my friend Tony at Albion Antiques on Golborne Road in London's Notting Hill. Danny added a sense of sparkle to this area by decorating the wall with this motif of stars. I used a delicate antique floral paper for the wall behind the sink to give it character.

Previous pages Across the landing from our room is our daughter Betty's room. Together we decided to paint this room an off-white to make the most of the light and also the tongue-and-groove panelling, which lines the walls and the vaulted ceiling. The nude portrait in oils on the radiator, from Hoof Brocante, was one of the first purchases I made when I visited this area.

Opposite I am forever collecting old fabrics and textiles, so much so that my cupboards and armoires in Somerset groan with the weight of them. It might strike some as an odd habit to have, but it has saved me so much money over the years by not buying fabric to order. Instead, I just rummage through my collection – it gives me such a sense of satisfaction when I'm able to transform an old curtain and restyle it into a new window covering, a blind/shade or a set of cushions.

Above This charming painted mirror hangs in the ensuite bathroom off the downstairs spare room. I found it at a flea market and, as is so often the case with these little finds, I purchased it simply because it caught my eye and appealed to me, with no concern for its value or its provenance. I just knew as soon as I saw it that I would find it a home and it works perfectly here, hanging above the basin.

Overleaf left A view of what will eventually become my laundry room, once I have finally decluttered it. I bought these beautiful encaustic Quinta Marron tiles from Bert & May. I love rich colours of the tiles: the chocolate brown and the red, set off by yellow and green detailing. And their wonderful pattern resembles a mosaic, which reminds of my travels in southern Spain and Morocco. The glass double doors, which I have lined with a fine door curtain, lead into the living space.

Overleaf right I don't believe that any room in a house has to be drab, not matter what its function, whether that's a downstairs loo or an office. And that applies to a utility room as well, as far as I am concerned. There's no reason why my laundry room shouldn't be pretty – especially given the fact that, as a mother of four, I spend a great deal of time in here. By hanging shelves in this room, I have also created much-needed storage space for my decorative collection of china, my vases and piles of surplus bedding.

Previous pages I have always been a great fan of "inside-out" living – creating areas in your garden that are just as inviting as the rooms within your home for relaxing, entertaining and dining. On the decking outside the living room I installed this beautiful Old Rocker swing seat from Odd Limited, which I then customized by adding a fringe to the canopy and tassel ties. I have covered its canvas cushions in a delightful candy stripe from Merchant & Mills. It is so comfortable that it's always a bit of race to see which of us can claim it first on a sunny day – though the dogs often seem to win that battle. I found the wrought-iron daybed on Ebay and like to dress it with old eiderdowns for extra comfort. The beautiful Moroccan pillow I found at Rae, in our neighbouring town of Rye, a vintage lifestyle store that specializes in textiles.

Left The guest cabin at the end of our garden is full of rustic charm and has a slightly magical feel to it, especially at night when it is lit up with twinkling lights strung across its porch. We inherited the old bathtub, which stands on the gravel outside of the cabin, from the previous owners. I was going to remove it but then realized that it was not only quite charming but would actually make quite a useful planter.

Opposite A lawned garden separates the main house from the cabin and here among the fruit trees I have created a sweet little dining area. The chairs and the vintage round oak garden table were all local finds.

The wonder of this property is, first and foremost, the light we get from the vast skies here on the south coast. I love deep colour, so much so that I am not afraid of painting a room a near-black, the bloodiest of reds or sumptuous purples and greens. However, it was clear that that wouldn't have worked in this setting. Instead, I wanted the original tongue and groove of the walls and ceilings to be painted in the palest of shades, the floors stripped back and the windows covered with the finest of lace panels to create shade but to allow that wondrous light in. From this starting point, I could then inject colour into the house using soft furnishings, bedding, rugs, lamps, paintings and tableware.

Left This fabulous 1950s-style parasol is from Sunbeam Jackie. Based in Penzance and run by the artist couple Charlie and Katy Napier, this company sells hand-crafted parasols made from an ash wood framework, with shades made from the prettiest of vintage fabrics. They can be made to order but I bought this one from the website, having fallen in love with it.

Opposite I love to collect tablecloths, be they lace or vintage silk with fringing. But out here I have used a crocheted cover. What is brilliant about this piece is that, while bringing a romantic feel to the table, its also machine washable – so I don't have to panic when there is a sudden downpour. I've owned this little pink ceramic jug for as long as I can remember and I love dressing tables with posies of flowers, even when we are eating alfresco.

The bedrooms would be cozy and would ooze that sense of delicious comfort that you want when you are away. The bathrooms would be pretty yet practical. Seating areas in the downstairs of the house would be enticing and, although the house isn't that big, I knew I wanted to maximize on the space we have for entertaining, be that inside or out.

Although I have collected a great many beautiful items over the years, from antiques to artworks, a lot of the pieces in the house have been put together on a shoestring. My love of flea markets and car-boot/yard sales never ceases and I am always in search of the next quirky find.

Left A view of the outside of the cabin with its decked terrace. When we started looking for our dream house by the sea, having an outside guest room was never on our wish list, but now that we have one I couldn't imagine life without it. Not only does it give us that additional space for when we have family and friends to stay, it also means that the main house does not feel too crowded.

Overleaf I wanted the two-bedroom cabin to be as be as cozy as possible, a place that I would happily stay in myself, with all the home comforts. For this reason, I updated the kitchen, installing a new oven and Swan fridge. I also invested in a sumptuous chocolate-brown velvet sofa from Soho Home, to which I added floral seat cushions to give it a twist. The kitchen chairs originally belonged to my eldest daughter, Daisy, who bought them from a store in Notting Hill called The End of the World. I always had my eye on them, so when she moved house recently, she kindly gifted them to me. I have since had them reupholstered in a floral Liberty print.

It might be a lamp, a battered chair or an old picture frame, or perhaps a set of china or tableware. Many of the unique vintage pieces that you can see in these photographs were actually sourced from the internet, via platforms such as Ebay, Etsy and Facebook Marketplace.

The one big investment I have made here, though, was in the kitchen, which is from DeVol. This is because we all love to cook and I knew that the kitchen would be the room in which we would be spending most of our time as a family. I used to have an aversion to fitted kitchens, preferring instead to have a mish-mash of reclaimed cupboards for that "rustic" look. To be honest, though, over the years we have all grown tired of banging our heads on doors that would hang off a single hinge whenever we reached for a plate, of cutlery/flatware drawers with no handles and of old ovens that simply wouldn't fire up. Although it is brand new, this kitchen still has a comfortable and lived-in feel, thanks to its Shaker-style design, which is in keeping with the age and look of the property. And most importantly of all, everything works.

Left I've painted the interior of the cabin in a soft, white linen shade from Lick, a newly established company that specializes in ecologically friendly paints. This was a slight departure for me, as I tend to rely on my go-to paint brands, but I'm always keen to do my bit for the planet and I couldn't be happier with the result. The pigment and the texture of the paint worked perfectly here. I found this charming kitchen shelf at Cosy Dot Company in Rye.

Overleaf To bring a sense warmth to the cabin's main bedroom and bathroom, I went for a palette of the palest peach tones. The antique French bed has been dressed in a canopy from Anthropologie. The cushion with my initials cross-stitched onto to it was a gift from a friend. The bright quirky floral mat hanging on the side of the tub was a find from Shepton Mallet flea market.

Opposite I love my striped windbreak, which was one of my first purchases when we bought the house. Not only does it protect us from the elements – rain, wind and sun – its bold colours and its canopy festooned with multicoloured pompoms give it an almost circus-like Big Top feel.

Previous pages and right The beach by the house is shingle but, when the tide is out, it exposes a wide expanse of soft, golden sand. On a sunny day, we will decamp from the house and make our way straight to the beach with flasks of tea and coffee and go for an early-morning swim. It's just a few minutes' walk to the sea, so we tend to come armed with furniture from the garden and a bundle of quilts and blankets to lie on. Come mid-morning I'll cycle to town on my beloved Pashley bike to pick up provisions for a picnic lunch and collect the newspapers, and then we will happily while away the day here until the sun goes down. This is my idea of heaven – the perfect day – and everything I envisioned when I used to dream, all those years ago, of my life by the sea.

Our house by the sea might have taken years to find and, even though there have been a few mountains to climb along the way, we have succeeded in making it our own within just a few months. I couldn't be happier with what we have achieved so far. There is still much for us to do – although it tends to make Danny wince whenever I say this to him. I can never quite leave a property alone, a trait that you could say is an occupational hazard of my work as a designer. But right now, Danny and I have what we have both always dreamed about – our own house by the sea.

Hut Heaven by the Sea

There is something so quintessentially British about a beach hut that appeals to my sense of nostalgia. Those rows of tiny huts, painted in a spectrum of the most mouthwatering sherbets and candy colours, make my heart sing and long before I found my house by the sea I always wanted to own one. In fact, if I hadn't found our home I would have happily settled for one of these.

Opposite A view of the interior of this magical beach hut that sits on the shingly shores of St Leonards-on-Sea. Its owners – the artists Claire Fletcher and Peter Quinnell – live in the historic fishing town of Hastings, just a 10-minute cycle away. This magical little cabin has a timeless feel to it, which I adore. Also, unlike so many beach huts I have been to, which are used simply for changing or storage, this is very much a home from home and is in use throughout the year. Claire describes it as almost an extension of their house – with the only difference being that the hut offers the most spectacular views of the sea. Paraffin lamps hanging from the rafters are essential when the sun sinks into the sea in the evening and they need light. A small zinc-topped table, covered here in a floral cloth, gives them just enough space for that early-morning cup of coffee. It is a place to eat and read or to play a board game when the heavens open.

Overleaf What makes this beach hut really special is that it is at the end of the row. This means that, unlike the other cabins, it has a dual aspect via windows at the front and on one side of the structure.

These simple single-storey structures are a legacy left to us by our Georgian and Victorian ancestors. Despite relishing the benefits of a restorative dip in the sea, they were quite prudish when it came to changing out of their high-necked, ankle-scuffing attire into their swimwear, so much so that they invented the "bathing machine" in the 1750s. This device, when wheeled down the sands by an attendant, would take bathers from the shore to the water without compromising their modesty. For more than a century, the machines were very popular among the wealthy and aristocratic – including Queen Victoria herself, who had one of her own on the Isle of Wight. In later years, that concept would evolve into the beach hut, still a place where you could change in comfort, but one that was more accessible to the masses. Not for that generation the struggle of wriggling out of your wet bathing suit behind a strategically placed towel.

That said, the beach hut has, thankfully, remained with us and is very much part of the landscape of our coastline. In fact, they are now so popular that in some areas there are long waiting lists for them and a modest beach hut can cost the same as a sturdy deposit on a one-bedroom apartment. Despite the expense, most beach huts are still used simply as a place to change, and as a storage space for seaside items – deckchairs, towels, buckets and spades, possibly a kettle and a couple of mugs – for holidaymakers and weekenders: nothing more than glorified, albeit prettily painted, sheds by the sea.

Opposite Even though the space is small, it's filled with so much character and personality. Flags hanging from the ceiling add colour to the vaulted wooden roof. A crocheted hanging – bought at a festival – brings colour to the doorway. An old wrought-iron hospital bed has been covered in the prettiest of throws, blankets and cushions and topped with a vintage eiderdown to make it all the more inviting. It is the perfect spot to settle down for an afternoon snooze, a good read or just to lazily admire this incredible view of the sea. Claire enjoys lounging here when she wants to relax. "If it's a good day, you can see as far as Eastbourne from here," she says with pride.

Right At the end of the bed, a tiny table groans under the weight of board games and reading matter. On top of all this sits a favourite childhood toy of the couple's daughter, Alice – a cuddly, much-loved and well-worn Barbapapa, who enjoys one of the best views of the sea from his perch.

But that is not the case when you visit the beach hut belonging to the artists Claire Fletcher and Peter Quinnell, in St Leonards-on-Sea. They own a house in Hastings but their hut, just a 10-minute cycle away from the town, is very much their home from home. This is the place they come to when they have time to swim, to relax, to eat, for a lungful of sea air and even to work, no matter what the season or the weather. And as soon as you walk into their hut, you can see that they have filled it with their innate sense of style, their personalities and so much love. If I were lucky enough to have a beach hut of my own, then Claire and Peter's would be my ideal.

It had aways been Claire's dream to have a place by the sea. She was raised in Northern Ireland, where her family home looked directly out on to the Belfast Lough, and so to be near water meant a lot to her. "I suppose having that at the end of your garden when you are a child spoilt me in some way," she laughs. "Peter says that, for as long as he can remember, I've always been chasing the sea and I can't deny it."

The couple met when they were at art school in London in the 1990s and moved to this part of the world after they graduated. They would go on to forge successful careers within the art world, Claire making a name for herself as an illustrator first and foremost, and Peter as a sculptor. Since they first moved here, they have always had a beach hut at their disposal, initially by renting them from the local council. Those huts were a welcome retreat from their life in town, and being so close to the sea gave them inspiration for a lot of their work.

Above left What I really love about this hut is that, even though it just a little retreat for the couple during the day, it is filled with so many homely touches that you could almost imagine that they live here full time. None of this is contrived, either. As Claire explains, over the years, items from their home in Hastings – books, toys, blankets, artworks – have seemed to "magically" find their way here. Above the daybed hangs this wonderful portrait, which the couple affectionately call *The Grumpy Girl*.

Above This bookshelf offers a truly eclectic choice of reading matter, ranging from books about the British seaside to this manual on *Very Advanced Driving*. "Like most things in the hut, I have no idea how the books have got here," says Claire, who admits that she is a real squirreller. "I just can't bring myself to throw anything away."

So when they saw an advertisement in a local newspaper for a beach hut for sale, on one the most unspoilt shingle beaches on the south coast, they simply couldn't resist this opportunity of a lifetime.

The hut has an old-worldliness to its design but it is actually a relatively new build, as with most of the huts you see dotted around our coastline. That is because, thanks to our cold and rainy climate, not to mention the salty sea winds, these structures rarely weather the elements for long. The wood eventually has to be replaced and the cladding will need to be restored and repainted every couple of years.

But when you first look at this enchanting hut, you'd be forgiven for assuming it was constructed long before you and I were born. That feeling extends into its interior, from the 1950s-style kitchenette and the paraffin lamps to the vintage furniture and the artworks. It is as though you have been transported back in time, which I love.

Above left Creative use of shelving affords Claire and Peter the storage they need and also allows them to create charming displays using their possessions – seen here is a collection of vintage books on the local area, a deck of playing cards and a trusty corkscrew – essential items for a rainy afternoon in the hut, one might imagine.

Above On this wall hangs a tambourine, onto which Claire has painted this wonderful picture of a mermaid – a motif that runs through much of her work as an illustrator. She likes to paint on tambourines not just because she enjoys their aesthetic qualities but also because the skin of the instrument serves as the perfect canvas for her artwork. The "Comic Cards" sign on the wall is one of Peter's finds. He loves to collect salvaged and vintage pieces like this that catch his eye.

Opposite Towards the back of the cabin the couple have installed this charming tiny retro kitchenette. I adore this mustard-coloured storage unit, so well-worn that the original red paintwork can be seen coming through, and I love that it has been left as it is. It has just enough room for the couple's basic pots and pans, as well as their plates and glasses. A 1950s-style cabinet gives them storage for cutlery and a surface for food preparation. Claire and Peter cook simple suppers using an ancient gas cylinder stove. Fresh fish, which they buy straight off the beach when the trawlers bring in the day's catch, is put on the barbecue. Above the window, a simple wooden shelf provides room for their collection of commemorative and souvenir mugs. Vintage floral curtains draped around the cabin window and the various little kitsch elements, such as this delightful kitten tray, bring character to this part of the hut.

This beach hut isn't just a folly for Claire and Peter – it is an extension of their home, and it is in constant use throughout the year. Claire will come here to sketch, either from a deckchair on the beach or from the old, wrought-iron hospital bed within the hut, which offers incredible sea views. Peter gains inspiration for his own work by being here and it is also where they spent precious time with their (now grown-up) daughter Alice when she was a little girl. When the sun is out, Claire and Peter swim, picnic and host barbecues. When the rain hits, they batten down the hatches and settle, with steaming cups of tea and a board game, at their zinc-topped table.

Above Flowers by the window in the living area frame the view of this beautiful beach in St Leonards-on-Sea, where an old fishing trawler lies abandoned and grounded on the shingle.

Opposite Peter, who creates wonderful art installations, loves to collect old salvaged signs such as this one advertising "Donuts", which is attached to the back of the door. I love their quirkiness and sense of whimsy.

Right The couple admit that its a battle to keep the hut shipshape and to protect it from the elements, especially if there has been a storm. They also have to repaint it every couple of years because of the corrosion caused by the damp, salty air, although I rather like the weathered look of this vibrant turquoise. Peter found these charming windows in a skip/ dumpster and installed them throughout the hut. The drop-down shutters are closed when the hut is empty or if there is a storm. This is very much a community – a little hamlet of huts – in which everyone knows each other and looks out for one another. On New Year's Eve it has become a tradition for everyone to gather on the beach, where a huge fire is lit. With a drink in hand, they look to the stars and out to sea while contemplating the year ahead.

Claire and Peter are on friendly terms with the owners of the neighbouring beach huts and enjoy belonging to this close-knit community. Technically, occupants are only allowed to use their huts by day, but Claire admits that she and Peter once broke the rules and spent a night here. "I'm not sure if we would do that again in a hurry," she admits with a smile. "It wasn't that comfortable and the amenities aren't great, as you'd imagine, but hearing the roar of the sea and the wind crashing against the shutters once we had locked ourselves in for the night – that was just magical."

Eclectic by the Sea

There is something truly magical about this Sussex property, which belongs to the artist Margot Crosby-Jones. Set far off the beaten track, it's so hidden away that you wouldn't know it existed unless you had been told how to find it. However, once you've navigated the dirt driveway, unlocking a series of gates along the way, you will soon find yourself in the midst of a fairytale.

Opposite They say that a kitchen is the heart of a home and this is never more true than here. Margot Crosby-Jones' kitchen is so full of character and warmth – if this room belonged to me, I doubt I'd ever want to leave. A long table, which Margot's late husband Mike owned for years, takes centre stage and I can imagine sitting here for long lunches and dinners, warmed by the Esse stove. The floor is made from garden pavers. The green chair was Mike's spot, where he would hold court when friends came over for ones of his legendary meals – he loved to cook and to entertain. An old chapel chair is a more recent find. Margot stores tide timetables in its shelf, where once there would have been hymn books. The dresser/hutch is one of her best-loved pieces of furniture is used to display her treasures.

It's almost as though you have climbed through a wardrobe and arrived in Narnia, such is its sense of otherworldliness. The first time I came here, I was mesmerized and felt that I had walked onto a movie set. This property is set in the most incredible garden, a vast plot of land, which is unusual for this part of the world. There are meadows of wild flowers, as well as more formal areas filled with fragrant rambling roses, daisy bushes and fruit trees. Sandy paths lead down to the sea.

But it is Margot's home itself that left me speechless when I first visited. It is not exactly a house, as it isn't just a single structure but a myriad of charming dwellings – outhouses, shepherds' huts, barns and workshops. It is like a tiny hamlet, situated right by the sea. This is a place that you can easily and happily get lost in.

Margot took the keys to the property on August 11, 1999, the same day that the UK witnessed a total solar eclipse. I'm a great believer in the power of the universe, and like her, I can't help but think positive forces were at work here, because it is a place so full of love and light. It was here that Margot spent so many happy years with her late husband, the acclaimed potter Michael Crosby-Jones.

Originally, it was the land that had drawn them here – the chestnut trees at the bottom of the garden, the fields and the proximity to the sea. The original house was a simple 1930s bungalow with two bedrooms, but Margot and Mike added to it over the years to create this rambling and extraordinary home.

Left An old-fashioned wooden laundry rail hangs from the corrugated metal ceiling, which is supported by two heavy beams. Margot's many baskets, which she has accumulated over the years, are also suspended from a beam in this room.

Opposite Everywhere you look in this house are examples of Mike's handiwork. I adore this little corner of the house with its hooks, cupboards and shelves – it's the perfect spot to store and display jugs/pitchers, vases and bowls. Margot's cat, Lucy, loves to climb up to the top shelf and settle down for a nap. The blue door leads out into a yard, which separates the main house from a tiny writer's cottage.

And what is so incredible about the renovation is that Mike did most of it himself. He might call on his friends for help from time to time, in exchange for a slice of his famous homity pie, but much of what you see here was created by his own fair hand. Long before we all became more environmentally aware, Mike was using salvaged materials to create outhouses, workshops, his pottery studio, sheds, a barn, chicken houses and a guest house called Reindeer Cottage. He was an acclaimed potter, but his skill at carpentry was above and beyond. "Mike hated being called an artist," says Margot. "He preferred to be described as an artisan. And his ethos was all about 'make do and mend'."

Margot and Mike were living the rural idyll. Both keen gardeners, in this smallholding they grew salads and vegetables, pumpkins and fruits in their kitchen garden and their polytunnel/hoop house: an abundance of produce that they would sell to their neighbours and friends. They had a menagerie of animals, too – chickens and ducks, sheep and two pigs, as well as their beloved cat Lucy. One has the feeling that neither of them could ever sit still. Mike would be up every morning at 5.20am in time for the Shipping Forecast on BBC Radio 4, somewhat appropriate listening when you live by the sea. He and Margot would tend to the house and garden before getting on with their respective work.

The kitchen garden is no more and has run wild, which is rather beautiful and appeals to my sensibilities. Clematis and honeysuckle climb with abandon. The outbuildings are now greening over with hops and roses. It may seem a strange comparison to make, but when I walk around here, I can't help but be reminded of the gardens of New Orleans – perhaps because this little slice of paradise, this secret garden, is so removed from what you normally find in these parts.

The main house is filled with so much warmth. I'm especially fond of the long, narrow kitchen with its vast stove and mismatched furniture, most of which they have owned for years. The dresser/hutch is a family heirloom, while the table, which I can imagine has been the centre of many a cheery gathering, was acquired during Mike's London years.

Above left Margot is a nature lover and she is forever collecting shells and feathers on walks and bringing them home with her. Window sills are adorned with these little treasures and finds, which bring the natural world indoors.

Above centre and right Margot is a keen and enthusiastic gardener, and her outdoor space is something to behold, filled with the most beautiful blooms from heady roses to sweet-smelling honeysuckles and jasmines. She loves to decorate the house with freshly cut flowers from the garden. Here, two tiny vases on a window ledge each hold a single clematis flower. It's a simple touch, but so charming.

Opposite I love the simplicity of this checked curtain, which is tied back with floral corsage. Shells and pebbles on the window ledge reflect the house's close proximity to the sea, which is easily accessible from the garden. The tall, straight pot is from Briglin, a 20th-century British studio pottery. Mike studied in Norway when he was learning his craft.

Left This charming wooden cabin, used as a guest bedroom, was built by Mike inside a woodshed. It is constructed out of used scaffold boards, inside and out, and was originally intended as a bedroom for Mike's son when he came to stay. It's affectionately known as "The Boardroom", but it has a cozy, Hobbit-like feel. I love the way Margot has filled it with homely touches, from the beautiful vintage quilt that adorns the bed to the oil paintings on the walls. The wooden beams are used as shelves and are lined with books and curios, such as this parasol. The pink checked blanket is from a shop called Endings, in Hastings, and was a gift from a friend.

Opposite This room is the perfect little retreat, a place to escape to. When it's not in use Margot comes here to read, relax, have a lie down or simply admire the garden from the window, which offers the perfect view of her majestic horse chestnut trees. The Crittall windows were salvaged from an old army camp, which was about to be demolished. Mike was so pleased with them that each Saturday, as the demolition progressed, he and Margot would go back for more windows for the house, which they brought home in an old Volkswagen Transporter. The only problem was that they were so heavy that they were at risk of toppling over on the journey home, so Margot would have to stand between them in the back of the van to stop them from breaking.

Bedrooms, though small, are charmingly cozy, and decorated with the most enchanting assortment of little pieces, which I feel tell the story of the couple's life together. Shelves and window sills are covered with tiny jars of freshly cut blooms, pots of shells that Margot has collected from the beach and, of course, an array of the most beautiful ceramics created by Mike and his friends.

This is a house of many rooms and many aspects. It is full of quirks, full of love and heart and soul and, as such, also full of stories. It is rare gem and I could happily give up everything to move here.

Above A view into the window of the cabin, where a beautiful porcelain vase on the writing desk is filled with sprigs of the most delicate, scented pale pink roses, hand-picked from Margot's garden.

Left There is a timeless sense of beauty to this garden with its picket fences – handcrafted by Mike, of course – and its little gates leading out into meadows and down to the beach. Seating areas for reading and relaxing are dotted throughout, and tables shaded by the boughs of trees are perfect for alfresco entertaining. To have such a luscious garden, so rich with flora and fauna, is rare in these parts, where the salty breezes and the quality of the soil can make it very challenging to create a perfect English garden. Somehow, out of some sort of alchemy, Margot has achieved this oasis.

Overleaf left A detail of the shed, with its distressed and weathered pink door and window frame, which Mike salvaged from his old wine store in a former home. This was originally the Duck House, home to Olive and Stanley, the Muscovy ducks and their many offspring.

Overleaf right In the workshop, we see a collection of Mike's pottery – glazed, decorated pots, tableware and cookware and these charming earthenware spotted pots, vessels, cups and bowls, all of which I covet. This is a house of so many stories and has such a sense of history, which is why I love it so much.

Beauty by the Sea

She may be one of the famous models in the world and a highly regarded photographer, but Helena Christensen believes she may have missed her true calling, such is her affinity with water. "I'm sure I was a mermaid in my former life, or maybe I am morphing into one for my next," she laughs. "I feel extremely connected to water in a way where I have a deep yearning to be near it."

Opposite The breathtaking panoramic view of the sea from Helena Christensen's beachfront cottage in Denmark is an image that she holds in her mind and takes with her wherever she goes. "Nothing beats this view anywhere in the world that I have been to," she says. "The magnificent sunsets, the birds flying back and forth, Sweden in the background and the lighthouse flickering in the dark at night, the sailboats floating by throughout the day, not to forget the occasional sightings of dolphins and porpoises. The beauty and the magic of it cannot be described in words." It is on this terrace that Helena likes to host her family and friends for lunches and dinners. The antique dining table has been decorated with shells, stones and pebbles, which Helena, who loves nature, enjoys collecting. The antique oil lamp is one of her treasures and makes a great centrepiece.

"It's like a calling for me," she continues. "I have to explore every lake or river or beach I pass, no matter where or what time of year it is."

Such is Helena's connection with the sea that 21 years ago, when she was pregnant with her son Mingus, she decided to buy a beautiful beach house just a couple of hours' drive from Copenhagen in her native Denmark. Her aim was to give her son a taste of the idyllic Scandinavian childhood she had experienced as a little girl, when she and her younger sister Anita would spend every summer at their grandparents' cottage near the beach in Denmark. Precious memories were created there; long walks along the coast, picking flowers in the forest, riding bikes to the beach, playing among the sand dunes and stopping for ice creams on the way home. And this is what she wanted to recreate for her son.

So when Helena set eyes this beautiful wooden house, which was built in 1929 near a tiny village on the coast, she felt as though she was coming home. The one-storey property is so close to the sea that you can see the ocean from any window – a discovery that made her feel "blessed". Set in an acre of land and surrounded by trees and rose bushes, the house has a sense of seclusion and yet it is only a short walk to the nearest village, which comprises just a handful of houses, a local restaurant and tapas bar and, most importantly of all, by her own admission, an ice-cream store.

Left On top of the mantelpiece in the living room, Helena has curated a collection of artefacts inherited from her late and much-loved grandparents. Her grandmother, to whom Helena was exceptionally close, was a seamstress. When she found this miniature mannequin on her travels she bought it to pay her homage to her, which made her grandmother smile. Also on the mantel is a portrait of her grandmother, who died when she was 100 years old. It is surrounded by candles and also a collection of her porcelain figurines. "I guess it's a bit of a shrine to her," she adds. "Anything that reminds me of her, I treasure."

Opposite Helena bought this beautiful old armoire from the wonderfully quirky Fil de Fir retro store in Copenhagen. She has filled it with some of her favourite things, including sculptures, linens and tablecloths. A keen collector of vintage clothing, she bought this dusky, silk dress in Paris many moons ago, and while she never wears it out these days, preferring to hang it from the wall or her furniture instead, it still fits. "I adore vintage clothing – the fact that others have lived their lives in those pieces." The artworks on the wall to the right of the armoire have a maritime theme. The large glass-framed piece is a collection of letters from sailors written to their loved ones at home.

The four-bedroom house needed little work and Helena was keen to retain its traditional look. The building has a maritime feel to it, so she installed additional porthole windows and made the most of its decked terrace that looks out to sea. "I wanted it to have the spirit of a ship," she explains. A garage was converted into a guest room so that family and friends can come to stay when Helena is here.

The views from the house are breathtaking and it is a quick walk down to the beach. In the summer the climate is warm, the water crystal clear and emerald green. "It's almost like swimming in Greece," she says.

Opposite Helena's bedroom is located towards the back of the property, away from the other rooms in the house for the sake of peace and tranquillity. Double French windows lead out into the garden, while windows on three walls let in not just light but the sound of the waves and the scent of salt water, so that on summer nights she almost feels as though she is sleeping outside. In winter she lights the wood-burning stove, which was built for her by a friend. The painting of the sailing boat is one of her most treasured possessions.

Above In the corner of Helena's room is a table covered with well-thumbed books. At night she loves to sit here and read by the stove. When the wood is lit and the glass door is closed, it makes her feel as if "witches are flying around in there". Over the fireplace is a still life of fruit and a carafe. "I love food and paintings of anything from our kitchens. I find it funny that in this day and age we take so many photos of our plates and instantly post them on Instagram. Back then, artists would spend days or weeks painting still lifes of their food to hang on their walls."

Left A detail of a small wall-mounted shelf in the guest bedroom. The bronze vase on the shelf was originally part of an old musical instrument. Helena loves to collect instruments – elsewhere in this room is a silver trumpet. Above the shelf is a charming portrait of an Edwardian woman. Helena has a vast collection of portraits of female subjects in her houses, both old and contemporary, because she finds women fascinating to look at. She also loves nude portraits of women dating from an era when "their bodies were soft and full and beautiful".

Opposite Helena's bedroom leads directly into this guest room, so it is only used when the house is completely full. That said, she has made it as cozy as possible. The antique wrought-iron bed has been dressed with a colourful assortment of pillows and cushions and the prettiest of bedspreads, which, with its faded tones of pink, burgundy and brown – one of her favourite colour combinations – Helena describes as "dark and poetic". She has added character to the tongue-and-groove panelled walls and brought in her personal style by hanging some of her favourite lace pieces from the exposed heating pipes. The sash window offers views over the garden.

In the morning, as soon as she wakes, Helena puts on her swimming costume, makes herself a cup of coffee and heads down to the beach with her beloved dog, Kuma. There she sits, watches the ocean and contemplates the day ahead before taking a sprint and, using the rocks on the shore as weights, she does a quick workout before plunging into the water for a morning swim.

Helena clearly loves the outdoor life, which the blissful location of the property suits so well. However, it is the interior of her home that really enchants me – and I use the word "home" wisely here.

You see, this isn't just a holiday house or villa that is merely opened up for guests in the summer months, only to be locked up again once the season is over. Instead, it is very much a family home filled with wonderful curios, objects and art that Helena has collected over the years, many of which she has inherited. Paintings line the walls, tables groan with books and an upright piano – a gift from her grandparents – takes prime position in the living room. Above all, Helena wants it to be cozy. Sofas are comfortable, the beds are layered with eiderdowns and blankets and the kitchen, although small, is very much the heart of the house, as she loves to cook. "I've always been an avid collector," Helena explains. "I have a huge affinity for anything antique or vintage – the craftsmanship and the history of old objects surpasses almost anything created today.

"It's very much a home – a cottage with a home inside. I see it as my bubble, it feels like it doesn't exist in real life or real time. When I'm here, it's just the house and the ocean – everything else is on pause."

Opposite The decked terrace boasts a 180-degree view of the coast. An iron gate takes you from the property down a winding pathway to the sea. Kuma, Helena's miniature Australian Shepherd dog, loves being here and she will often sit beside the gate throughout the day, waiting patiently for her mistress to take her down to the beach.

Above left The house was built in 1929 and although Helena made a couple of changes to the property, such as creating a guesthouse and installing the French windows that lead out onto the terrace, she was keen to preserve the maritime feel of the building. A bank of wild rose bushes separates the house from the beach.

Above right Other than giving it a lick of paint and installing a metal worksurface, Helena, who loves to cook, kept the simple kitchen as it was when she first bought the property. The porthole window looks out onto the sea and a small side garden, which is filled with an abundance of wild strawberries and herbs. The stove faces into the living room and to its right is an upright pianette that Helena's grandparents bought for when she was just eight years old. In the evening, there is nothing more she likes to do than prepare a meal while her son Mingus sits at the keyboard and plays for her as she "stirs the pots".

Carriage Life by the Sea

I have always had a passion for railway travel and by that I'm not referring to the all-too-tedious commute that we make these days. For me, it is about that golden age of steam travel, of Pullman carriages, of the midnight sleeper, the restaurant car where breakfast didn't consist of a soggy sandwich and styrofoam cup of tea but was served from a table laid with linen cloths and silverware.

Opposite A view of the exterior of the 19th-century railway carriage on The Ridge in East Sussex, which has been converted into a family home. Its owners, the Rankin family, have not just lovingly restored the carriage but have built around it to create a stunning five-bedroom house. Each cabin in the carriage has direct access from the old train doors onto this tranquil porch area, which the family have filled with vintage garden furniture. The family often gather here in the mornings for lazy breakfasts and in the evening for tea and drinks. Though it is just a few minutes' walk from the carriage to beach, this area feels secluded and private. It is protected from the weather – be that sunshine or rain – by the galvanized roof overhead. From the upstairs balcony, there are breathtaking views of the beach and the sea.

Of course, it depended on what class you were in, but in my mind that's when train travel was at its most glamorous and romantic. It is the reason that when it came to my hen party, rather than book a dinner at a swanky restaurant, my girlfriends and I boarded a British Pullman train and took a day trip from London to Bath.

So imagine my delight when, while I was out walking the dogs one morning on Winchelsea Beach in Sussex, I caught sight of a beautiful 19th-century railway carriage that had been converted into a house. Two of my great passions – houses and trains – were rolled into one. This stunning conversion, in a spot known as The Ridge, belongs to Elsbeth Turnbull and her husband Derek Rankin.

The Rankins are not the only family in this area to have converted a disused carriage into a home. Along this coastline you will see many abandoned 19th-century train carriages that have been repurposed. After the war, many were recommissioned to provide accommodation for the returning soldiers and the local workforce. But what I really love about this carriage, in particular, is the love and the care its new owners have put into its restoration – although that isn't that surprising when you consider that Derek is a highly acclaimed RIBA architect.

When the Rankins and their three children first came to The Ridge seven years ago, they were looking for a family home, not a railway carriage. But they immediately fell in love with it and realized its potential. That said, they had to work out a way to make it into a home.

Opposite The train's Guard's Room has been transformed into a cozy area for the family and doubles up as a spare room. The vaulted ceiling creates not only a feeling of height in this room but also lets in the light through the additional skylight. The daybed has been covered in a Liberty-print patchwork quilt and an abundance of cushions. The carriage's original wooden floors have been restored and covered in vintage rugs for warmth. Elsbeth bought the charming little Napoleon chair at the Ardingly Antiques Fair and draped it with a sheepskin throw. The driftwood sculpture of a star was a gift from a local artist.

Originally, the site consisted of two 9m/30ft-long carriages. Derek saw that by losing one wagon and freeing up the surrounding land, he could construct a house around the remaining carriage. It was built in 1890, according to a plaque on a wooden beam in the Guard's Room, and now forms the aspect of the house that looks out of to sea. Behind it, Derek has built a two-storey addition to house the family and guests.

The carriage itself is divided into three cabins: an office, a child's bedroom and the Guard's Room. The latter, used as a snug and spare bedroom, benefits from a taller, vaulted roof and skylight.

Above A pink cyclamen on the ledge of the daybed in the Guard's Room is planted in a beautiful handmade and hand-painted pot from the Gillshaw Pottery, based in Rye. This small studio was founded by two ceramicists, who take inspiration for their designs from walks across the East Sussex countryside and coastline. The Rankins have restored the carriage's distinctive original teak drop-down windows to their former glory.

CARRIAGE LIFE BY THE SEA 109

All the original wooden floors have been brought back to their former glory, the classic teak drop-down windows still have their 19th-century brass fittings and train doors open out from each of the three cabins onto the porch area.

Though they were keen to keep the palette of the carriage as neutral as possible to make the most of the wonderful coastal light, Elsbeth has added colour and character to the interiors. She runs the Rye Bay Beach School, a magical educational enterprise that teaches children all about coastal living, from shrimping and crabbing to beach cleaning, and even runs circus classes. She has filled the carriage with brightly coloured soft furnishings and unusual vintage finds, most of which have been sourced locally.

The glamour of train travel is back – even if this carriage, now brought back to life, has reached its final destination.

Above left and right Throughout the carriage Elsbeth has added some playful nods to her work at the Rye Bay Beach School, which teaches children about the beach from tides to the environment. When the children aren't fishing, crabbing, shrimping or getting involved in beach-cleaning schemes, they also spend their time learning circus skills: taking courses in trapeze work, making juggling balls or designing costumes. The Harlequin tutu here is one of my own designs from my childrenswear line, the other items here have been collected by Elsbeth from her productions.

Opposite The beautiful shell picture frames on the ledge of the daybed were sourced from a wonderful shop called Merchant 57 in Hastings. The vintage rose-print cushion is from the Cosy Dot Company and the surrounding pillows are from the Nordic textile brand Projektityyny.

Right The second room in the cabin belongs to the couple's youngest daughter, Skye. The vintage metal bedframe is from the Three French Hens, a brocante-style emporium that specializes in all things French from homewares to garden furnishings. The bed has been dressed in linens and muslins and finished with a mosquito net that hangs above the bedhead. The aim here was to create a room that was light, airy and pretty. The half-moon night light hanging above the cabin windows was a gift from Skye's godfather. Skye was very much involved in the decoration of her bedroom. She chose the colour of the paintwork for the walls – French Gray from Farrow and Ball – and she also, at the age of ten, decided she wanted a mural on the walls, which she painted herself.

Above Handmade bunting and glitter balls festoon the trees in the garden – remnants from a party. Elsbeth admits that she probably should have taken them down the following day, but she just finds them too charming.

Opposite left A detail of the white flowers that Skye painted by hand on the wall behind her bed. Each flower was individually painted by the 10-year-old and, according to her mother, the mural was completely her idea.

Opposite right The house is filled with vintage glass and enamel vases that Elsbeth collects. All the flowers come from family's garden.

Overleaf This pretty painted mirror is from the Lion Street Store, an antique shop in Rye. It sits on a chest of drawers that has belonged to Elsbeth since childhood. The original carriage woodwork has been stripped down and painted in natural hues throughout the wagon's interior.

Page 118 In a paddock outside of the carriage live two horses named Clover and Smoke. The family has a menagerie of animals that includes dogs, rabbits and hens.

Page 119 There is nothing more that the family likes to do together than to spend time on the beach. Think flasks of tea, Sunday papers and just enjoying the view and the weather on a good day. They are all keen swimmers. Derek and their eldest daughter Hettie recently took part in a relay across the Channel, during which they raised thousands of pounds for charity.

Pale and Interesting by the Sea

Set in three acres of garden and meadow fields, Foster House has a distinctly New England feel, with its boarded exterior, wrap-around veranda, whitewashed tongue-and-groove interior walls and painted timber ceilings. However, we aren't in Maine, Connecticut or New Hampshire. We are, in fact, in Romney Marsh, a low-lying coastal area of natural beauty in Kent.

Opposite The whole house feels light and airy, thanks to Atlanta and Dave's signature pale palette. They have injected hints of colour with their clever use of accessories and furniture. In this bedroom, a quirky antique wrought-iron bed, painted in a vibrant turquoise and dressed in pastel and floral bedding, immediately draws the eye. A gilt chair, which doubles up as a nightstand, adds a touch of glamour. Light floods in from the garden doors, which are adorned with a soft lace curtain, and from the skylight above. I love the way they have used the structure of this room, its supports and beams, to create shelving space for a few carefully chosen decorative pieces.

Overleaf Across the three-acre site, the couple have built a series of outbuildings and cabins – all designed by Dave, who has a background in set design. Some are used as locations for shoots, while others are rented out as holiday lets, but this space belongs to Atlanta, who uses it as her design room. I love the simplicity of the white wooden cabin-style seating. Double doors lead out onto a tiny deck. This is perfect spot to bask in the sunshine and admire the beautiful view over the meadow field.

This period property, built in 1840, is home to the much-fêted design duo Atlanta Bartlett and Dave Coote. As you approach the house from its garden, which is filled with an abundance of rose bushes and fruit trees, you can't help but be beguiled by what the couple have created.

Painted in the chalkiest of whites throughout and minimally but artfully furnished with beautiful pieces and artefacts, this is a place of wonder. Light floods in through the sash windows and skylights, bouncing off antique mirrors and high vaulted and pitched ceilings. A vast family kitchen, its warming range cooker set into a hearth, welcomes you in. Bedrooms, though simply styled, are inviting.

It is almost as though you have walked in onto a movie set, and you could be forgiven for that initial thought, because the couple both have roots in set design. Dave, now a hugely respected furniture and product designer, began his career in the film industry in New Zealand and has a history of designing sets for photo shoots. Atlanta, meanwhile, cut her teeth working in the magazine industry – at first for *Homes & Gardens*, before going freelance as an interiors stylist and art directing for leading publications both in the UK and abroad.

Today, this prolific pair, along with a myriad of other ventures, run The Beach Studios, an agency that represents stylish locations in London and the south-east. Their client list is impressive, but arguably the jewel in their portfolio is their own property, which can be hired out for shoots, along with the many cabins and outbuildings on their land.

Previous pages left The window ledge above the bench in Atlanta's studio is decorated with a charming ceramic teapot and glass jars filled with shells that she has collected from the beach at the end of their garden.

Previous pages right The house is covered with vases and jugs/pitchers of homegrown flowers from the garden. I adore the way these blowsy pink booms are arranged in this antique blue and white china bowl. They bring in an explosion of colour.

Opposite This is the entrance to Atlanta's studio. There is something so romantic about this scene, especially the stable-style doorway and the roses and ramblers that grow around it. The garden has many distinct areas, from the meadow to the more formal garden outside the house. This little patch of gravel is surrounded by beds of the sweetest wild flowers.

Above Mirrored glitterballs hang from the boughs of the trees in the garden, creating a sense of magic.

But although Foster House is a go-to location for filming and photography, at its heart it is very much a family home. The husband-and-wife team moved here in 2005 from London when Atlanta was pregnant with the third of their four children. The idea behind the move from the city was simple – they wanted and needed more space for their creative work and the thought of raising their children by the coast had obvious appeal.

Fortunately, they didn't have to look far when it came to finding their dream property – they bought Foster House from Atlanta's father, an artist, who was looking to move on. That said, they had their work cut out. As charming as this classic Kent clapboard cottage was before they moved in, they were going to have to add to the house both to accommodate their growing family and to make room for their work.

If ever there was a couple suited to the task ahead, then it was these two, with their mutual love of design, interiors and gardens. Though their specialisms lie in different fields – Atlanta leaning towards textiles, art direction and styling, while Dave's strengths are in furniture and structural design – their skill sets complement each other. "We are very much Yin and Yang," she says. "And that's why it works so well." What they do share is a fundamental vision when it comes to style. Their mantra is simple: "Keep it Simple, Keep it Relaxed, Keep it Real."

Atlanta and Dave set to work on the structure of the house first, transforming the original 19th-century cottage, where her father had lived, into a sprawling six-bedroom, two-storey house.

The building work has been so sympathetically executed and is so in keeping with the spirit and the character of the property that, unless you had seen it in its former incarnation, it simply wouldn't occur to you that some parts of the house are actually newly built additions. But it is what they have created within the interior of the house which, in my opinion, is the best showcase of their design skills and creative flair.

Above Light flows through Atlanta's spacious studio thanks to the skylights and the vast barn doors, which lead out into the the garden. This is the most heavenly place to work and I can't help but envy it. A raised table is the perfect place for her to work on her designs. Paintings, ornaments and curios on the shelves add character and personality to the room. A set of hooks in the hallway, which leads out onto the deck, is home to Atlanta's collection of hats and shawls. Baskets line the beautiful wooden floor.

There is a subtle balance to the house. It has a minimalist style to it and yet it oozes comfort. It's uncluttered and yet you couldn't describe it as being sparsely decorated, for it is full of character. Every item has been lovingly chosen and has a story behind it. It is stylish in terms of its design, and yet deceptively practical, as well.

The interiors of the house are painted from top to bottom in shades of white and other muted tones, but the rooms do not feel cold or austere. This is thanks to the couple's clever use of chalky paints and lime washes, which create a sense of warmth.

The pale, restrained palette seen throughout the house is a signature look for Atlanta and Dave, who have written a series of bestselling books on the subject. They also run a successful online shop, Pale & Interesting, from which they sell their beautifully designed furniture, a line of home and garden wares, lighting and a range of stylish accessories, both vintage and contemporary.

"We believe a home should first and foremost be a place for living. Homes that have been designed as status symbols or follow current trends religiously have never appealed to us," Atlanta explains.

Above The couple have created this wonderful entertaining space on the lawn, close to the main house. I love that the long table is situated under the shade of the magnificent apple tree, which serves as a natural parasol

Opposite The veranda adds to the colonial feel of the property and plays on the inside-out style of living. Vintage wrought-iron beds have been transformed into cozy sitting areas and an old leather trunk is a great place to rest a tray of ice-cold drinks or a cup of coffee. Shade is provided by the slate-tiled roof overhead.

As Atlanta walks me through this remarkable house, she explains the values that have always guided the couple's creative work, including the decoration of their own home. "What interests us is the human element, where simple pleasures are celebrated, imperfection is encouraged and self-expression is crucial. A well-designed home should be practical, of course, but to us the emotional and sensual impact of an interior ranks above everything else. Maximizing daylight is one example. Tactile surfaces, honest materials, choosing vintage over newly made and handcrafted items over mass-produced are the building blocks of our ethos."

Opposite Atlanta and Dave love to decorate their home with organic and natural objects – shells, branches, driftwood or even vast piles of logs that tower from floor to ceiling. Here on the porch wall, they have mounted a set of vintage antlers and I love the way they have been playfully decorated with glitterballs and flowers.

Above There are two caravans on the property – a 1960s Airstream trailer and this refurbished caravan from the 1950s. Both are available for hire as locations for film and photo shoots via the couple's agency, The Beach Studios.

Previous pages The family love to gather round this scrubbed kitchen table, which they have owned for years, especially when Atlanta and Dave's four children are all at home – their eldest is 21, their youngest 10. The room is large but what gives it an even greater sense of space is the incredible double-height vaulted ceiling, which here has been festooned in streamers – the remnants of Atlanta's recent birthday party. Raising the ceiling was one of the first structural changes the couple made to the house when they took it on. The white marble counters that surround the sink were reclaimed from a dairy. The range cooker occupies the original fireplace, which has been tiled in a white brick design. Above it is a wonderful old sign, advertising hot tea, which the couple found on one of their trips to India.

Right A vase of flowers on the kitchen table. They say that Kent is "the garden of England". Out here on the coast, gardeners face a constant battle with the elements, and yet Atlanta and Dave have created a magical plot filled with the headiest of blooms.

Dave and Atlanta are deeply environmentally aware, and not just when it comes to their own way of life. It is a commitment that extends to all aspects of their work, from the items they design and source for their Pale & Interesting boutique to the cabins that Dave has created on their land, which are rented out as holiday lets.

"Alongside minimizing our carbon footprint through the use of sustainable materials, recycling and repairing wherever possible, it's our aim to create homes that have integrity and soul," says Atlanta.

As a self-confessed hoarder, I'm rather in awe of this simplicity and serenity of this house, which to me seems so perfect. Atlanta laughs this off and reminds me that she is a busy working mother of four. The family also have a dog and they love to entertain. "I'm also quite practical – so yes, we have painted floors, but they are actually easier to maintain than anything else. You can sweep away the sand and mop away the mud. Good storage is also key." Still, I wonder how she does it.

Previous pages left One of the many outbuildings in the grounds of Foster House is a corrugated metal structure known as the Log Cabin, which was designed by Dave. Inside, an old leather armchair is in keeping with the weathered, patinated look of the steel panels that line the vaulted ceiling and two of the interior walls.

Previous pages right Large windows on the outside of the Log Cabin allow the daylight to flood in. Pale & Interesting is the name of Atlanta and Dave's online boutique and is also the title of one of their bestselling books about their interior-design aesthetic.

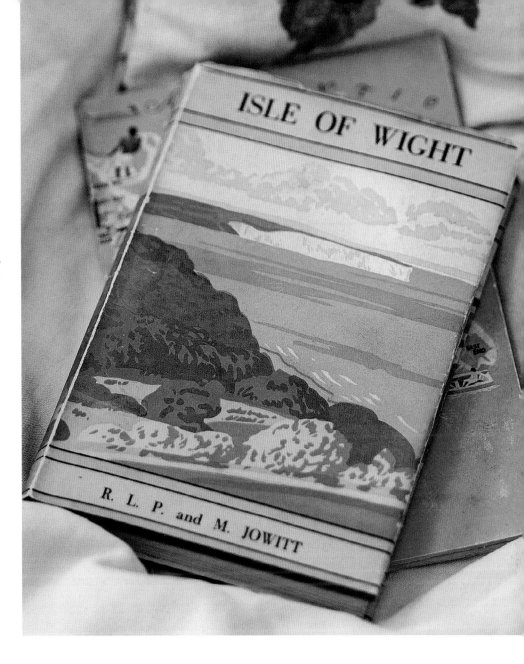

To me, this house by the sea, surrounded by its outbuildings and charming cabins and set in the middle of its stunning gardens and meadows, is sheer perfection just as it is. However, I get the impression, while I am talking to Atlanta, that she and Dave still regard it as a work in progress. She agrees that this is the case. "I doubt we will ever stop working on it or get to a stage when we feel it's completely finished. I guess that's an occupational hazard, being designers," she explains. "Life changes, it evolves and morphs. A home should grow and improve with age."

Opposite The Log Cabin is named for the fact that two of its walls are clad in rough-cut timber logs. These bring an element of the rustic into this space, in contrast with the industrial corrugated steel. A gilt-framed, cane-backed sofa is dressed with cushions and throws in a mix of colours, patterns and textures.

Above This vintage book about the Isle of Wight dates from the 1950s and has a charming illustration on the front cover.

Wandering by the Sea

There is a sense of otherworldliness about Dungeness, a headland at the southernmost point of Kent. With its vast shingle beach – the largest in Europe – the stark, desert-like landscape is punctuated by abandoned fishing boats and weathered shacks. Overshadowed by the looming towers of a disused nuclear power plant, it is at once hauntingly bleak and yet incredibly beautiful.

Opposite When you first set foot on Dungeness, you could almost be forgiven for thinking that you had walked onto a film set. With its Wild West landscape, its marshlands and its vast shingle beach scattered with abandoned fishing trawlers, there is something outlandish and yet incredibly beautiful about this place. As you walk around the stark headland, it can be hard to believe that you are actually in Kent, the county known as the Garden of England.

Overleaf Dungeness is a designated National Nature Reserve, rich and diverse in its wildlife. It is home to more than 600 species of flora. Hardy sea plants grow in clusters throughout the shingle, but I find that what makes my heart sing when I walk here in the spring and summer months is the wild flowers, especially the poppies. They bring a burst of colour to this otherwise desolate landscape.

Artists and writers have long been drawn to Dungeness for its extraordinary and inspiring light. Nature enthusiasts come to explore the numerous trails around this remarkable landscape, which boasts more than 600 types of plants that flourish here in the wetlands and wildflower meadows of Romney Marsh. It is a bird lover's paradise, too, with its dazzling array of domestic and migratory species, which can be observed from numerous hides dotted across the promontory. Tourists flock here to take a ride on the world's smallest passenger railway and to take in the view from the top of the old lighthouse.

And then, of course, there is Prospect Cottage. It was in this weather-beaten, coal-black Victorian dwelling that Derek Jarman set up home in the 1980s. The avant-garde director, writer, set designer and artist remained there until his death in 1994. With a John Donne quotation still adorning an outside wall, nowadays the house attracts not only film lovers but horticulturists. They come to pay homage to the incredible garden Jarman created here, including the sculptures he made out of sea plants, pebbles, driftwood and scrap metal.

There are many reasons why I am drawn to Dungeness, among them the wildlife and the landscape – I even have a strange affection for the power plant. I also come here for the food; the fish and chips, to be precise. When Danny asked what I wanted to do for my birthday last year I knew exactly where we were headed: to the Snack Shack, where we sat on the beach and feasted on fried fish baps and lobster rolls.

Opposite The Dungeness Fish Hut is a family-run fishmonger that is very popular with the locals, who flock here to buy their sustainably caught seafood. The family's two trawlers, launched from the shingle, head out to sea each morning, weather and seasons permitting – and return later to bring home the freshest of fish, which can be bought directly from the hut.

Left Although many of the old, wooden boats that line the coast here have been abandoned and sit eerily upon the shore like ghost ships, Dungeness is still very much a working fishing town and it is said to serve some of the best fish and chips in the British Isles.

Below Sitting beside the Fish Hut is its sister project, the Snack Shack, housed in a converted caravan. Here the owners serve the day's catch – turbot, lemon sole, bass or whatever has come out of the sea that morning – grilled to perfection and served in a warm bap with a side order of fries. In the summer months we come here for lobster and crab rolls and Mexican fish wraps, and in the winter for the piping hot smoked chowder. With your lunch in hand, pull up an old-fashioned deckchair, admire the view and tuck in.

Vintage by the Sea

When I visit France, there are few things I love more than spending a morning at a brocante. These wonderful local markets can be found all over the country, with tables groaning with anything from high-end antiques to funny little curios. Some people travel to France for the food, the wine, the culture, the climate, but for me it is all about the brocante – that is my guilty pleasure.

Opposite Hoof Brocante on Romney Marsh is a treasure trove of the most delectable finds, from furniture, paintings and high-end antiques to more affordable items such as tableware, enamels and linens. Everything is carefully curated by Tara Franklin and Adi Higham, who source their wares mainly from France – the home of the brocante. In this room, a French 19th-century wooden chest has been covered in the prettiest of floral papers. During that era the French had a passion for covering their boxes, books and chests in these divine decorative papers. The painting of the trawler, behind the antique model boat, is a watercolour on board and dates back to the 1930s. In each room Tara, with her expert eye, has created these seemingly effortless yet wonderful tableaux to showcase the wares.

I can while away hours sifting through piles of monogrammed linen sheets and pretty patterned eiderdowns, filling my basket with vintage glassware and china, and haggling for a piece of painted furniture or an old pastis bottle. I don't know what it is about the French, but they even make their bric-a-brac seem chic and glamorous.

It has been a while since we went to France, perhaps because on our last trip to Paris, we visited a flea market where I fell in love with a beautiful 1920s fringed floor lamp. Having made my purchase, I made poor Danny carry it back home on the Eurostar, for which he has never really forgiven me. So it was much to my delight (and his relief) that after moving here I discovered that I would not need to cross the Channel to get my brocante fix, as there is one right on my doorstep.

Hoof Brocante is set in an old RAF base on Romney Marsh, Kent, and is run by antique dealers Tara Franklin and Adrian Higham. They met a decade ago when Tara started buying off Adi. They soon became friends, then business partners and that turned into something more.

Tara has a keen eye for textiles, paintings and decorative antiques. Adi, a larger-than-life character, is well known within the trade and has found fame as an expert on the BBC's popular show *The Bidding Room*. He is much more into the "boys' stuff" as Tara puts it, with a laugh. "Anything mechanical or industrial, anything to do with cars – I never know what he's going to bring through the door next. A toy rocket, a car, a full-size 1950s firetruck. He recently bought a Dalek."

Their specializations might seem worlds apart, but what they do share is their love of all things French and hence their vision to open their own brocante here on the south coast of England nine years ago.

Some might have raised an eyebrow at the idea of bringing such a quintessentially French concept to Britain, where people are more used to either formal antique shops and auction rooms or car-boot/yard sales, but Tara and Adi were convinced they were onto something, and they certainly have their credentials in that field. Not only do the couple own property in France, but Adi lived there for more than 20 years. He and Tara are equally well known on both sides of the Channel.

Hoof is an Aladdin's cave of all things covetable. The space is cavernous in size, beautifully dressed and filled to the brim with all things wonderful. You could spend hours browsing one room before realizing that you have another six to explore.

Above left The entrance to Hoof Brocante, which is situated on a former RAF base in Kent. Spread across seven rooms, plus an outdoor space, the cavernous showroom has become a go-to destination for anyone with a passion for all things French.

Above right Vintage vases, antique glassware and ornate china will bring a touch of faded glamour to any dining table. Here a beautiful planter takes centre stage. It actually dates back to the 1980s and is made of concrete but has been weathered over time and so looks as though it came from an earlier era.

Opposite A 19th-century French salon chair is upholstered in a faded blue velvet. The charming 1930s vintage cushion, embroidered with the the words 'Fragrant Memories', was found in Cognac but actually hails from the US seaside port of Bar Harbor, in Maine.

There is 19th-century painted furniture: chests, armoires, screens, boudoir dressing tables and button chairs. You will also find rolls of French vintage fabric – toiles de Jouy, velvets and linens – plus whimsical ornaments, glassware and china. You could walk in here and come out with a fine antique or you could simply set your heart on a set of enamel plates and you would still leave happy. And that is before you make it outside into the sea air and encounter a haul of terracotta pots, urns and garden furniture – everything you could ever want for your outside space, including pieces you might not really need but inevitably convince yourself you do.

I once came in looking for a small piece of fabric and left with the most incredible painting – a nude, which now hangs in my sitting room. This is very much my idea of faded glamour and it is also by the sea – albeit not on the French coast but situated here in Kent.

Overleaf On the left is a detail of a beautiful early-19th-century toile de Jouy. To the right, another salon chair is upholstered with an embroidered design. On its seat is a toile bedspread and a yard of antique brocade. When Tanya and Adi first set up the brocante, they allocated just one room to showcase their collection of textiles. This quickly expanded, such was the demand for these wonderful fabrics not just from locals like myself, but from suppliers and designers as well.

Pages 154–155 This antique screen is one of Tara's favourite finds, but it was not until she had to wrestle it into her truck that she realized how heavy it was. It is covered in a divine 19th-century fabric inspired by Les Indiennes. Attached to it is a portrait of a lady in oils on unstretched canvas. Tara is uncertain of its provenance but loves it for its sheer glamour.

Retreat by the Sea

When I first embarked on my quest to find my house by the sea, I quickly realized that I would have to find a place to stay on the south coast. And, of course, there are many wonderful places to stay in this part of world, from the grand Edwardian and Victorian hotels that grace the grand promenades of local resorts to the simpler, more affordable guesthouses by the sea.

Opposite I could happily spend most of my days and evenings sitting at this table and admiring this incredible view of the beach and the pier. Opened to the public in 1872, Hastings Pier is something of a tourist attraction, especially in the high season. From here, with a cup of coffee in hand, you can admire it in its full glory without getting caught up in the throng. I love the fact that the window has been left uncovered so as not to distract from the sheer spectacle of this vista. The enamel-topped kitchen table has been dressed in a lace cloth. From the ceiling hangs a beautiful 1940s chandelier. This light fitting would have originally been mounted on the ceiling, but here it has been dropped it down to create a more romantic feel. Its chain has been entwined with a dusky pink ribbon to soften it.

In fact I was spoilt for choice and any one of those would have suited me, but when a friend suggested that I stay in her flat in the heart of St Leonards-on-Sea I leapt at the chance. Not only was it an area that I was keen to explore, being a vibrant seaside town filled with restaurants, cafes and, even more appealing, a wealth of antique shops and vintage stores, but I liked the idea of living like a local during this time rather than feeling like a tourist.

I'd been warned that the it was a long walk up to the apartment, which is situated on the top floor of a vast, gloriously handsome Victorian building on the seafront, but that wasn't what took my breath away. What made me gasp, as I opened the door of this charming two-bedroom home, was the view. From the kitchen window you have a completely uninterrupted view of Hastings' historic pier and directly out to sea. Now I could understand why the owner had opted to live at the top of the building rather than take an apartment below.

When it comes to my own properties, I am guilty of being a bit of hoarder – as Danny often reminds me whenever I bring more "stuff", as he calls it, into the home. I hate throwing things out, especially when they have meaning to me, but I sometimes secretly yearn to live in a space where less is more, and that's what you find here.

The interior's charm lies in its sheer simplicity, which was a priority for the owner. As someone who travels the world for work, her aim was to find a retreat by the sea where she could relax and recharge.

Right The apartment is situated on the top floor of this magnificent Victorian building, on the seafront of St Leonards. It stands on the corner of the town's picturesque Warrior Square and, while it might be a long climb up to the top of this imposing building, it is worth it for the views alone – not just of the sea, but of the square's beautiful rose garden as well.

Overleaf The simplicity of this room creates a feeling of peace and tranquillity with its white walls and painted floorboards. The original Victorian grate has come away from the wall and is propped up on bricks for now, but I feel this only adds to the charm of this room. The bed, which is covered in bedding from Rachel Ashwell's Shabby Chic Petticoat Collection, has a romantic feel as a result of all those ruffles and tiers of cotton and lace. The painted nightstand was a local find. The fringed 1920s-style bedside lamp with its peach silk shade adds a dash of colour to the room.

Opposite The second bedroom has been painted in the softest of lilacs. The gilt-framed French Louis XV-style bed, which has been upholstered in a delicate floral damask, was found in St Leonards, as were the matching bedside tables and the lamps, which give this room a grander feel. From this room you can lie in bed and admire the view. The pretty pink ruffled pillows and the floral quilt again came from Rachel Ashwell, another friend of the owner, who often stays at the apartment when she is need of an English seaside break.

The bedrooms are spacious and light, and while sparsely furnished, with just the bare necessities for a good night's sleep, they are also luxurious, with beds covered in sumptuous linens, quilts and pillows.

A wall that once separated the kitchen from the sitting room has been knocked down to create a light-filled, open-plan living space. The original floorboards have been stripped and the walls painted in pale hues to make the most of the extraordinary light that floods through the windows, which wrap around the three aspects of the apartment. This heavenly apartment is really my idea of the perfect seaside retreat – an inspiring place to escape to.

Above This is a detail of one of my own lace curtain panels from my decorative collection. I've been designing these hand-dyed cotton lace panels for over 20 years now. Back in the day it was my solution to cover the windows of my London house, allowing privacy but not at the expense of light. I left this panel here as a house gift and chose this fuchsia-pink design because I thought it would complement the pink and the sage green of the blossoms on the charming floral bedspread.

Tequila by the Sea

One of my favourite discoveries during my time in St Leonards was Cactus Hound, a wonderfully colourful saloon-style tequila and cocktail bar set back from the main drag of the town on the Western Road. For those who know me well, this might come as something of a surprise, as I don't drink. But I'm not here for the tequila – I'm here to admire the beautiful interior.

Opposite I love the use of bold colours in this room. The combination of deep red and rich yellow creates a sense of warmth and intimacy, while the fun dark green painted stripes give the effect of a dado rail/chair rail. The furniture was sourced from flea markets and vintage stores around the area, and I adore the fact that none of it matches. Sofas and armchairs upholstered in velvets and old fabrics add to the saloon feel of the bar. Vintage table lamps and sconces with silk shades cast a soft light over the lounge area.

Looking at the magnificent floor-to-ceiling bar – the centrepiece of the room – dark varnished wooden floors, slatted shutters and antique furniture dotted throughout, you would be forgiven for assuming that this establishment had been here for decades – centuries, even. But in truth Cactus Hound has actually only been existence in since 2018 – and to me that is the genius of this design project.

When the owner first stumbled across the site, it was nothing more than a shell, a forlorn empty space set in a corner building on a street away from the beaten track. But rather than being deterred by its state or its location, the owner used both to their advantage. The fact that the ground floor of the building was derelict gave them a blank canvas to work with, and that it was slightly away from the more touristy parts of the town gave it a more dive-like vibe.

And that was their aim. They wanted Cactus Hound to have the feel of an old-school saloon lounge, like the ones you might have found in Los Angeles back in the day. They wanted to attract not just tourists but also locals throughout the year. There would be live music. It would be a place for a quiet evening drink as well as for late-night partying. There would be cocktails and, above all, there would be tequila – a staggering 45 varieties of tequila and mezcal, to be precise.

From the outset, the owner was adamant that, despite being a tequila bar, Cactus Hound should not look like a clichéd Mexican-themed venue, and so they put a lot of thought and care into its design.

Previous pages Although it looks like an antique, the bar was actually designed for a film set and was a bargain find for the owner. Having treated and stained the woodwork once they took possession of it, they installed a zinc counter and created another unit for the dresser/hutch to take it to ceiling height. This provided more shelving space to showcase the bar's many varieties of tequila, mezcal and other spirits. The pretty chandeliers above the bar are actually made from plastic, not glass, and were another bargain, costing just under £50 for all three. Towards the back of the room is a small stage for live gigs and open mic nights. In the basement is a recording studio, which is rented out to local musicians.

Opposite When it came to selecting the furniture for Cactus Hound, the remit was simple. Everything needed to look old, even if it wasn't, and preferably a little weathered to contribute to the saloon vibe of the bar. However, above all it needed to be robust – this is a bar after all. These slatted shutters are a clever addition. Not only are they in keeping with the overall style of the bar but they keep the sun out in the height of summer and the heat in during the winter months.

To create a sense of warmth, the walls have been painted in the richest of colours. A deep oxblood surrounds the base of the room and a rich yellow meets it in the middle, separated by two dark green stripes that give the effect of a dado rail/chair rail. The ceiling has been painted in a glossy shade of tobacco, evoking an era when smoking wasn't frowned upon.

The building's original vast, goldfish-bowl plate windows are shielded by beautiful, weathered-looking shutters, which not only add to the saloon-bar feel but keep the heat in and, of course, prying eyes out.

But it is the story of the bar itself that I really love. Like most people, I assumed it must be an antique, perhaps reclaimed from another establishment at vast expense. But it is in fact a prop that was designed for a movie and had been gathering dust in a basement. The owner bought it from the production company for just £500.

The Cactus Hound is well worth a visit, whether you are here for a refreshing cocktail on a summer's evening after a day by the sea, or something stronger to warm your cockles on a winter's night. Or, if like me, you simply want to immerse yourself in the ambience of its interior.

Rock-n-Roll by the Sea

I first met Carl Barât and Pete Doherty, frontmen and founders of indie rock band The Libertines, around 20 years ago when Danny and I went to see them at Cherry Jam in London. They later supported Danny's band. There was such a buzz about them at the time and, by getting to know them over the next few years, I got a taste of their world.

Opposite A view of one of the seven bedrooms at The Albion Rooms, the Margate hotel owned by the indie rock band The Libertines. This room – the Emily Dickinson Room – is affectionately referred to by the staff here as "Pete's Room" because this is the room in which frontman Pete Doherty stayed, with his menagerie of dogs, while the hotel was being done up. The wallpaper on the back wall was inspired by a scrap of a drawing of a scantily dressed Victorian lady. This was digitally reproduced by the wallpaper specialist John Mark to create a toile-effect wallcovering.

Overleaf The hotel is on the Eastern Esplanade of the town and has wonderful views of the Thanet coast. The interior designer Rhiannon Sussex, an old friend of Libertine Carl Barât's who helped the band with the renovations, found this magnificent 1930s brass bed in a local antiques market in Margate. The other walls of the Emily Dickinson room have been painted in a rich caramel, the windows picked out in gold and dressed with black velvet curtains. Rhiannon was keen that the room should feel sumptuous and luxurious. The heart artwork is one of Pete's doodles, which he graffitied on the wall before the room was decorated. Eager to preserve it, Rhiannon had it framed and then had the room painted around the piece.

There would be impromptu gigs at their flat, to which anyone and everyone was invited, and I knew then that they not only had a sense of fun but also style. Think vintage flags, battered leather sofas and fringed lamps. Their flat was known as the Albion Rooms. The band have now bestowed the same name on their latest venture, a five-storey hotel in a Victorian terrace in the seaside town of Margate. It is a fitting nod to the naughtiness of the Noughties.

But The Albion Rooms isn't just a hotel, it's a Warholian-style "factory", complete with a state-of-the-art recording studio and a beautiful bar where they host poetry and comedy nights and jamming sessions. Where people come, in their words, "to relax, write and record by the sea" or stay in one of the hotel's seven bedrooms.

The band never set out to be hoteliers. "We never saw ourselves following in the footsteps of Basil Fawlty," says Carl with a laugh. "What we wanted was to create a haven for anyone with a creative persuasion. But it soon transpired that, while being fun, it was far from economically viable." And so the hotel was born.

The Libertines did not have any hands-on hospitality experience prior to The Albion Rooms, but they certainly knew their stuff. Having spent the best part of 20 years on the road, they have a finely honed sense of what makes a hotel special. Carl explains the formula: "Good food and drinks 24/7, late checkouts, art events and a sea view."

Previous pages left The mirror in the Emily Dickinson Room was purchased from a vintage shop in Margate called Lost Property, where the team sourced many other items for the hotel. It has been customized with gold paint to fit in with the opulent scheme.

Previous pages right This ornate, lacquered oriental table with mother-of-pearl inlay was found in Pete's lock-up, which Rhiannon describes as the most unbelievable treasure trove of beautiful furniture and items that the frontman had collected over the years but never used. That said, the pieces had to be painstakingly cleaned before the team could begin to see what would work in the hotel.

Opposite The upstairs suite at The Albion Rooms is called The Loft. Here a window is dressed the most of opulent of plush, velvet curtains by Anna Hayman. The floor lamp was found on the street, revived and then adorned with this wonderful 1920s-style double-fringed lampshade, which was also made by Anna.

Above A detail of a wall-mounted shelf in the Emily Dickinson Room, which has been dressed with quirky curios, from the gold cherub plant pot to the old box of playing cards. The whimsical Art Deco split-head antiqued bookends came from Rockett St George and the Corona typewriter belongs to Pete, who has a vast collection of them.

Overleaf left The communal areas of the hotel follow a palette of red, black and gold, taking inspiration from the military-style jackets that the band used to wear on stage. In the hallway, the walls are painted in an off-black from Farrow & Ball and the magnificent red carpet runner is fastened down with gold clips. The orange jug/pitcher in the foreground is a beautiful piece of 1960s studio pottery.

Overleaf right Rhiannon found this stunning 1930s cranberry-coloured glass chandelier online and knew it would bring a sense of decadence and glamour to the staircase. However, when it arrived in the post, she realised to her dismay that she was going to have to construct it herself by individually beading the glass droplets. An arduous task, but one that was worth it in the end.

Above This framed photograph of Carl and Pete in the early days of their career was taken by the acclaimed music photographer Roger Sargent. It shows them admiring their matching Libertines tattoos. There are many subtle nods to the band throughout the hotel, from framed scribbled lyrics to artworks and photographs. However, the band were adamant that The Albion Rooms shouldn't be a hall of fame drowned out by memorabilia, and should still have a rock-n-roll vibe.

Opposite A glowing crucifix, in red and pink, is reflected in a limited-edition Sex Pistols print. This four-foot-high neon design was specially commissioned for the hotel from the local neon artist Stuart Snape. Set against a black wall in an upstairs hallway of the hotel, it brings a sense of drama to the space.

But the hotel is more than just that. Rock-n-roll as it might be with its punk-noir decor, the building has been beautifully restored. In its former life, the hotel had been deemed "the worst guesthouse in Kent", as the band will happily tell you, so this was quite a feat. When they took the keys, everything in the hotel was "sticky and old" – the carpets were filthy, the floorboards spongy. The spa downstairs was a group of sauna rooms and hot tubs, which resembled a "sad swingers' club". These were ripped out with chainsaws to make way for the studio.

The luxurious bedrooms are filled with art and antiques, and downstairs is an acclaimed restaurant and bar. Carl has recently added to The Albion Rooms venture by teaming up with chef Gizzi Erskine to open a café, which pays homage to the seaside caffs of yesteryear. There is no avocado toast on the menu at the Love Café. You come here for a proper fry-up, a deep-filled sandwich or an old-fashioned sundae.

Opposite The Arcady Coffee House is where hotel guests and locals meet for breakfast, brunch and cocktails and admire the views of the coastline from the bay windows. The russet wall lends warmth to the room and the leather porter's chair was another vintage find.

Margate has always attracted creatives – JMW Turner declared that the skies in this region were "the loveliest in all Europe", and TS Eliot wrote part of *The Waste Land* here. It is also where Tracey Emin grew up. This stretch of coastline was once England's riviera but in the last century, it fell into decline. Margate became a ghostly promenade of fish-and-chip shops, amusement arcades and empty guesthouses.

But since the opening of the Turner Contemporary gallery in 2011, Margate has enjoyed a rejuvenation and has upped its game. Not least with the opening of this beautifully designed, achingly cool, creative hub of an establishment.

Above The back wall of the Arcady Coffee House has been papered in Hollywood Palm, a bold design by Martyn Lawrence Bullard from Cole & Son. The shelves behind the bar are home to a collection of vintage ice buckets and glassware. The chairs surrounding the tables have been spray painted in black and gold. The overall effect of the decoration is to give the room a warm and decadent ambience.

Opposite The exterior of the hotel has been painted in a deep charcoal, the balconies in gilt and the hotel's neon sign is a vibrant red, once again reflecting the colours of the band's jackets. The sign was made by Stuart Snape, who based the design on Carl's handwriting. The hanging sign for The Waste Land – the hotel's downstairs bar, in which the band host poetry, comedy and live music nights – was designed by a local child.

Above *Mrs Booth, the Shell Lady of Margate* is a 3.5m/12ft-tall bronze statue is by the artist Ann Carrington, based on the kitsch shell sculptures you find in the tourist shops around this seaside town. Sophia Booth, a widow, was JMW Turner's landlady at the boarding house where he resided when he came to Margate and later became his lover after the death of his wife. Situated on the Harbour Arm of Margate Old Town, she looks out onto the best views of the Thanet skies and coastline, which inspired so many of Turner's paintings.

Elegance by the Sea

What is it about the call of the sea? That's the question that stylist and entrepreneur Mitzi Lorenz asked herself following an early morning meditation on the beach in Hastings, East Sussex. She had only meant to spend a couple of days in the fishing town as a break from her hectic schedule. She was due to return to London at the end of the week but, as the sun rose over the sea that morning, she knew she wasn't going back.

Opposite When Mitzi first took possession of the Regency villa on West Hill, in the Old Town of Hastings, there was little for her to do in terms of structural renovation. Her aim was to make the best of the original features of the house, to keep it very simple and uncluttered and to play on the grandeur of the building's architecture. Here a beautiful gilt-framed sofa, from the French Depot in St Leonards-on-Sea, has been covered in a vibrant pink damask. The wall behind is lined with the prettiest vintage floral wallpaper. Throughout the house, the floors have been stripped of their carpets to reveal the wooden boards underneath, which have been restored and painted. Hastings is famous for its shops selling a variety of antiques and bric-a-brac, so aside from the furniture that Mitzi brought from her home in London, most of the items in the villa have been sourced in the local area.

Within just a matter of weeks, Mitzi had signed the deeds of one of the most beautiful houses in Hastings; a five-storey, Grade II-listed Regency villa right in the heart of the historic Old Town.

It's fair to say that a few eyebrows were raised when she told her friends she was quitting the Big Smoke for life in a seaside town. As one of the most acclaimed stylists of her generation, Mitzi was very much part of the London scene. As a teenager she quit school and co-founded Buffalo, a collective of artists, stylists, designers, musicians and photographers. Together, in the late Eighties and early Nineties, they turned the mainstream media on its head, cultivating an exciting new movement of creativity. But Mitzi knew she was making the right move. "There was something so magical about the area," she explains. "The light here is special. In the winter it's dramatic, and in the summer it's simply beautiful."

The house itself, which dates back to the early 19th century, is steeped in history. This was the location of the old Hastings Pottery – its kiln still remains, and at the base of the house is a multitude of historic smugglers' caves.

Situated at the top of West Hill and built into its sandstone bedrock, the house offers breathtaking views over the bay and the rooftops of the town. Vaulted ceilings and vast arched windows not only allow the light to flood in but also give the villa a sense of grandeur.

Left Mitzi has transformed this reception room into her design studio where she is currently working on a collection of women's and men's clothing. She has placed her industrial sewing machine in the bay window, which looks out over the south coast, to make the most of the spectacular light. She likes to be in this room early in the morning to watch the sun rise over the fishing boats, and at night to meditate in the moonlight.

Overleaf left A detail of the hallway and one of the staircases in the five-storey house. Here, Mitzi has stripped back the stairs and restored them back to their former glory. The use of light-coloured paints on the bannister and the walls here makes the most of the original features of the house. Although the villa is a sanctuary for Mitzi – a space in which she can relax, take stock and focus on her work – it is also very much a place to entertain and she has thrown some legendary parties here.

Overleaf right Mitzi found this charming blue French vase at London's Portobello Road antiques market and she has had it for as long as she can remember. One of her most cherished possessions, it sits in the fireplace of one of the main bedrooms.

Previous pages This is one of the four bedrooms in the house. Mitzi describes it as a work in progress, "Though I rather love the fact that it's unfinished," she says. "It adds to its charm." She was planning to redecorate it completely. However, when she had stripped the walls of their paintwork, she found that she loved the raw look of the plaster and so decided to leave it as it was. The antique French bed, which she has yet to pair with a mattress, she found in St Leonards. On the mantel is a William Blake print inspired by Dante's *Inferno* and a photograph of the actress Nastassja Kinski. The shaded lamp on the floor is another find from Portobello Road.

Opposite When she isn't working or entertaining, Mitzi likes to spend her downtime relaxing in this extraordinarily beautiful 27m/90ft-long orangery. It features a fish pool, surrounded by tropical plants and vines, under a 9m/30ft-high glass roof. Many of the plant species in here are incredibly rare. On summer afternoons, Mitzi escapes the heat by taking a siesta on this traditional Indian charpoy daybed. She has created seating areas throughout the orangery using finds from India and Afghanistan and local markets, including this charming blue wicker chair and a pair of elephant stools, which she uses as side tables.

But it is the 27m/90ft-long orangery, which wraps around the western side of the house, that is arguably the most extraordinary feature of the property. Filled with grapevines, palms, banana trees, orchids and other tropical plants, it is said that this glasshouse, one of the oldest in the country, was where Captain Cook stored his horticultural finds from voyages before they were transported to Kew Gardens.

In the summer, when the weather is good, Mitzi retreats to the formal lawned garden with its sea views where, as a "committed sun worshipper", she sunbathes, often naked. "That's the joy of being at the top of the hill – you aren't overlooked," she says with a laugh.

Above In a corner of the oranger, Mitzi has installed this stunning 3m/10ft-tall Chinese porcelain vase. She has positioned it next to one of the original fireplaces in the glasshouse. The sandstone bedrock of the hill is exposed on this side of the house, which once served as a pottery. At one time, this part of the building was also used as a smokery for the local fishermen's hauls. The house is a truly magical place. "I had no idea I would find a place like this when I first came to Hastings," says Mitzi. "I sometimes think it's as if it chose me."

Shabby Chic by the Ocean

On our final trip to the sea I am venturing further afield, taking you on a journey to Malibu on the west coast of America. Here, in an enchanted garden filled with bougainvilleas, hydrangeas, scented rose bushes and banks of lavender, lies a charming, light-filled beach house. This beautiful coastal retreat is home to the designer, author and entrepreneur Rachel Ashwell.

Opposite Rachel's Malibu home has a guest house that is affectionately known as "The Train" because of its long, skinny structure. She designed it for her daughter Lily, who, when she was a teenager, wanted some space of her own away from the main house. A raised queen-size, platform bed has plenty of room for storage underneath. Bolsters, covered in fabrics from Rachel's Shabby Chic collection, are used to transform the bed into a sofa during the day. The cotton rugs can easily be shaken out to remove any traces of sand.

Overleaf The house is set in a beautiful lawned garden, with beds of lavender lining the pathways. Rachel always fills her houses with flowers. Despite the salty climate, the soil here is rich, so she has an abundance of blooms to play with – among them are scented roses, camellias and hydrangeas. She loves to dry her laundry out here in the sea breeze.

If you were to envisage your perfect home on the coast, then this could well be it. Enclosed within its magical garden, a few strides from the ocean, it basks in the warm Californian sunshine. But location aside, the house itself is so artfully designed that, in my mind, you could transport it to any coast in the world, and it would still be perfect.

This won't come as a surprise for anyone familiar with Rachel's work. Known for her eye and her innate sense of style, she was an early champion of the vintage look, which she called "shabby chic". This phrase entered the lexicon of interior design, summing up an aesthetic in which old meets new. Rachel would later adopt Shabby Chic as the name of her successful lifestyle brand.

Rachel has a passion for all things vintage and retro, which she expresses in her design work, but without ever compromising on comfort. It's an alchemy that is actually quite hard to achieve, but she makes it look effortless – and her Malibu home is no exception.

In many ways, this single-storey, four-bedroom property is a house of contradictions. It's spacious but can also be cozy, thanks to Rachel's clever use of sliding barn doors to partition off the open-plan living space. The decoration is minimal but not without character, as she has lovingly curated the house around her "forever pieces" – a mirrored dressing table, a freestanding Venetian mirror, an Italian cabinet and her collection of old needlework samplers, my favourite being the one that reads: "God Bless This Home".

Previous pages left When she isn't working, Rachel loves to entertain family and friends. This rustic old table has been dressed with a lace runner and is surrounded by a set of pretty French chairs, which have become the inspiration for designs in her own collection of dining-room furniture. Like me, Rachel loves to collect vintage plates. Ever resourceful, knowing that their designs won't withstand the heat of a dishwasher, she uses them as placemats instead, with more robust modern plates on top. Vintage napkins have been dyed by hand to give them a new lease of life.

Previous pages right The kitchen is simple in design, yet spacious enough to cater for a full house. This is one of Rachel's favourite rooms – the counter, with its eclectic collection of chairs and stools, is the perfect place to gather for "snacking and chatting". If she wants privacy, she simply slides across the vast barn door that divides this room from the living area.

Right This vast L-shaped, sectional sofa is one Rachel's own designs. Called the Bloomsbury, it is covered in the palest of pastels and furnished with the softest of cushions. Rachel has made something of a name for herself when it comes to sofa design. She and I first met more than a decade ago at her shop in Notting Hill, where I bought one of her sofas covered in red velvet. When Rachel first started her business, it came off the back of designing a slip cover for her own sofa that was machine washable – at the time, she was the mother of two young children, with sticky fingers and sandy feet, so practicality was an imperative.

The palette of the house is pale throughout, but then Rachel will inject colour into a room with a beautiful glass lamp or jewel-toned porcelain pot. Beds are draped in the most romantic of ruffles, which you never want to get out of. Sofas, in pastel hues, are so plump and inviting that you just want to dive into them for a long nap after a day at the beach.

Rachel and I met over a decade ago and bonded over our mutual love of all things vintage. That said, we would both agree that our styles differ – with her love of pale interiors, Rachel sometimes balks at my preferred palette of blacks, purples, reds and greens. In turn, I marvel at the fact that she can live without clutter. Rachel has spent most of her adult life living on the coast. This was one of the reasons why I not only asked her to art direct this book, but also turned to her for inspiration when it came to creating my own house by the sea.

Above Rachel believes that bedrooms should be beautiful yet cozy. Here, her bed is dressed in a romantic flurry of the softest of white cotton bedding from her Petticoat collection. A large Venetian mirror is propped up against the wall to the left. "I'm quite loathe to hang things – I guess you could say I have commitment issues," she says with a laugh. The white gloss painted floors give off the perfect sheen.

Opposite In Rachel's bathroom, she has used these wonderful matt, hexagonal tiles to give a modern twist on a classic theme. A generously sized freestanding sink, with its plumbing left exposed, has been softened by the tasselled silk shades of the wall lights above, which sit on either side of a vintage mirror. This room is her sanctuary – a place to relax and enjoy a long hot soak after a day at the beach.

Stockists

Pearl Lowe
www.pearllowe.co.uk
IG: @pearllowe

ANTIQUES & VINTAGE

AG Hendy & Co
www.aghendy.com
+44 (0)1424 447171

Arbon Interiors
www.arbon-interiors.
mysupadupa.com
+44 (0)20 8960 9787

Brocante Living
www.brocanteliving.co.uk

Cosy Dot Company
www.cosy.company
+44 (0)7778 197892

Dairy House Antiques
www.dairyhouseantiques.com
+44 (0)1747 853317

Dig Haüshizzle
www.dig-haushizzle.co.uk

The French Depot
www.thefrenchdepot.com
+44 (0)1424 423703

French General Trading
www.frenchgeneraltrading.co.uk
+44 (0)1373 466155

The French House
www.thefrenchhouse.co.uk
+44 (0)20 7371 7573

Hand of Glory
www.handofgloryantiques.com
+44 (0)7867 305451

Hawk & Dove
www.hawkanddove.co.uk

Hoof Brocante
www.hoofbrocante.com
+44 (0)7722 217397

Jasper Jacks
www.jasperjacks.com
+44 (0)7905 204247

La Marette Brocante
+44 (0)7729 347006
IG: @la_marette_brocante

Lark Vintage
www.larkvintage.co.uk
+44 (0)7988 615686

Les Couilles du Chien
www.lescouillesduchien.com
+44 (0)20 8968 0099

Marchand Antiques
www.marchandantiques.co.uk
+44 (0)7889 540789

Merchant 57
+44 (0)7967 637540
IG: @hastingsmerchant57

Old Albion
+44 (0)7879 051362
IG: @oldalbion

P&T Antiques
www.pt-antiques.co.uk

Pale & Interesting
www.paleandinteresting.com
+44 (0)1797 344077

Pigeonniere
www.pigeonniere.com
+44 (0)7747 064329

Rag & Bone
ragandbonebristol.com
+44 (0)7577 118978

The Rye Emporium
www.theryeemporium.com
+44 (0)7802 437188

Three Angels
www.threeangelsbrighton.com
+44 (0)1273 958975

Urbanraid Trading
IG: @urbanraidtrading

RECLAMATION & SALVAGE

Frome Reclamation
www.fromerec.co.uk

Glastonbury Reclamation
www.glastonburyreclamation.
co.uk

Symonds Salvage
www.symondssalvage.co.uk

Wells Reclamation
www.wellsreclamation.com

FURNITURE, LIGHTING & ACCESSORIES

Baileys Home
www.baileyshome.com
+44 (0)1989 561931

FRP Homestore
FRPhomestore.com
IG: @frphomestore

Graham and Green
www.grahamandgreen.co.uk
+44 (0)1225 418200

House of Hackney
www.houseofhackney.com
+44 (0)20 7739 3901

Odd Limited
www.oddlimited.com
+44 (0)1865 416836

Preen by Thornton Bregazzi
www.preenbythornton
bregazzi.com
+44 (0)20 8964 9995

Rachel Ashwell – Shabby Chic
www.shabbychic.com
+1 888 393 5875
IG: @rachelashwell

Rae
raelifestyle.com

Sera of London
www.seraoflondon.com
+44 (0)7977 534115

Rothschild & Bickers
www.rothschildbickers.com
+44 (0)20 7359 5817

SHOP
+44 (0)1424 438159
IG: @shopnormanroad

Soho Home
www.sohohome.com
IG: @sohohome

The Stripes Company
www.thestripescompany.com
+44 (0)1244 336387

Toast
www.toa.st
+44 (0)333 400 5200

KITCHENS & BATHROOMS

Artisans of Devises
artisansofdevizes.com
+44 (0)20 3302 9996

Bert & May
www.bertandmay.com
+44 (0)20 7352 4904

Bertazonni
uk.bertazzoni.com
+44 (0)1244 987366

Burlington
burlingtonbathrooms.com
+44 (0)1322 473222

DeVol
www.devolkitchens.co.uk
+44 (0)1509 261000

Fisher & Paykel
www.fisherpaykel.com
+44 (0)8000 886605

Swan
shop.swan-brand.co.uk
+44 (0)333 220 6050

WALLPAPER, PAINT, TEXTILES & TRIMMINGS

The Cloth Shop
www.theclothshop.net
+44 (0)20 8968 6001

Coco & Wolf
www.cocoandwolf.com
+44 (0)1749 871219

Farrow & Ball
www.farrow-ball.com
+44 (0)1202 876141

Lick
www.lick.com

Little Greene
www.littlegreene.com
+44 (0)845 880 5855

Morris & Co and Sanderson
sandersondesigngroup.com
+44 (0)20 3457 5862

Piglet in Bed
www.pigletinbed.com

Index

Page numbers in *italics* refer to the illustrations and their captions

Acknowledgments

I want to thank my wonderful husband Danny for being there for me and putting up with my eclectic taste and ongoing hoarding – I knew the clutter would come to good use one day!

Thanks to our four lovely kids, Daisy, Alfie, Frankie and Betty, for allowing me to decorate and re-decorate their bedrooms and never really complaining too much about it, even though I know they would much rather have had posters all over their walls.

Thanks to my gorgeous Mum for being my confidante and a constant source of inspiration to me and to my darling Zoe for being such a wonderful friend through all these years.

Thank you to Anita for being my absolute rock at home and to Rachel Ashwell for your guidance, great taste and friendship.

Thank you to Dave Watts for making everything look so beautiful and being such a dream to work with, and to Natasha Garnett for the months of hard work you have put into this book – I will miss our daily chats.

Thanks to Cindy Richards for having the faith in me to create another book, I am eternally grateful and I wish you all the happiness on your new path. Thank you Sally, once again, for your perfect design skills. And thanks to Sophie Devlin and Annabel Morgan for being so patient and getting the book finished.

Thanks to the homeowners for allowing us into your enchanting places.

I could not have made this book without all of you.

Pearl Lowe